# THE **CRUCIFIED** LIFESTYLE

9 Practical Principles for the
**Cross-Centered Life**

Dustin Renz
Foreword by Dick Brogden

# THE **CRUCIFIED** LIFESTYLE

## 9 Practical Principles for the
**Cross-Centered Life**

Dustin Renz

THE CRUCIFIED LIFESTYLE
Copyright © 2024 by Dustin Renz.

All rights reserved. No part of this book may be used or reproduced in any manner whatsoever without written permission except in the case of brief quotations embodied in critical articles or reviews, except as provided by United States of America copyright law.

For more information, please contact MAKE WAY MINISTRIES online at: www.makewayministries.com

Library of Congress Control Number: 2023923982
Renz, Dustin 1983-
The Crucified Lifestyle: Nine Practical Principles for the Cross-Centered Life
First Edition: January 2024
Make Way Ministries

Unless otherwise noted, Scripture quotations are taken from the NEW KING JAMES VERSION®. Copyright © 1982 by Thomas Nelson. Used by permission. All rights reserved.

ISBN: 978-0-9979060-5-9

Printed in the United States of America.
10 9 8 7 6 5 4 3 2 1

OTHER TRANSLATIONS AND PARAPHRASES USED
(in order of appearance)

Scripture quotations are taken from the HOLY BIBLE, NEW INTERNATIONAL VERSION®, NIV®. Copyright © 1973, 1978, 1984, 2011 by Biblica, Inc.™ Used by permission of Zondervan. All rights reserved worldwide. www.zondervan.com The "NIV" and "New International Version" are trademarks registered in the United States Patent and Trademark Office by Biblica, Inc.™

Scripture quotations noted NLT are taken from the HOLY BIBLE: NEW LIVING TRANSLATION. Copyright © 1996. Used by permission of Tyndale House Publishers, Inc, Wheaton, IL 60189. All rights reserved.

Scripture quotations from the COMMON ENGLISH BIBLE. © Copyright 2011 COMMON ENGLISH BIBLE. All rights reserved. Used by permission. (www.CommonEnglishBible.com).

Scripture quotations are from the ESV® Bible (The Holy Bible, English Standard Version®), © 2001 by Crossway, a publishing ministry of Good News Publishers. Used by permission. All rights reserved. The ESV text may not be quoted in any publication made available to the public by a Creative Commons license. The ESV may not be translated in whole or in part into any other language.

# ACKNOWLEDGMENTS

I am very grateful to everyone who has provided valuable insight and direction on this project. I want to express my gratitude for the contributions of the following people by name:

Thank you to my wife, Brittany, whose editing and proofreading skills have helped make the message of this book more effectively communicated. Also, for being a continuous listening ear during writing projects like this.

Thank you to Nate Danser, who helped to clarify the main concept for this book, which gave me the ability to bring a much more concise message.

Thank you to Shy Renz, for helping get the manuscript into its final form and for all of your encouragement along the way.

Thank you to Jonathan Willetts, for your willingness to do the cover design for the book. I so appreciate the skills that God has given you.

Thank you to Dina Mangarella, for your proofreading and editing input.

A special thanks Delbert Hill and Josh McCamey, two of my ministry board members, who have helped spur me on along the journey.

Each of your input on this project has been invaluable to me.

# DEDICATION

I dedicate this book to my three Dutch brothers in Christ, Arjan Baan, Leander Janse and Martin Penning. This book would not have been written without your invitation to teach on The Crucified Life at the Gospel Mission Bible School in 2017. Getting to know you and spending time together over the years has been an iron sharpening iron experience, and I value our friendship in the Lord. May He continue to bless your efforts as you reach the Netherlands and the nations of the world with the Gospel of Jesus Christ.

# TABLE OF CONTENTS

Foreword..................................................................................................13
Introduction...........................................................................................19

## Section One: A Crucified Lifestyle
1. What is the Crucified Lifestyle?..................................................25
2. The Path of Much Resistance ....................................................41

## Section Two: A Victorious Lifestyle
3. Crucified to Sin .............................................................................57
4. Crucified to the World .................................................................73
5. Crucified to the Opinions of People..........................................91

## Section Three: A Surrendered Lifestyle
6. Surrendering Our Personal Rights .........................................107
7. Surrendering Our Plans ............................................................125
8. Surrendering Our Finances .....................................................141

## Section Four: A Disciplined Lifestyle
9. The Discipline of Self-Denial ...................................................161
10. The Discipline of Maturity .....................................................177
11. The Discipline of Intimacy ....................................................195

Conclusion ............................................................................................211

Appendix................................................................................................219
Notes......................................................................................................223

# FOREWORD

In 2007, we stood on the shores of an Islamic sea wondering how on earth the Gospel could reach (at that time) 1.6 billion precious to God Muslims – now even more. We concluded that it could only happen if we lived as if we had already died, which is just a current way to try and capture an ancient truth. It is just an alternative way to describe the crucified life. For the crucified life is always centered on others. We live dead, so that the dead may live.

G. Campbell Morgan put it this way: *"The cross is always personal, self-emptying, in order to the serving and saving of others. You and I know nothing of the cross so long as our suffering is personal merely…our personal sorrows do not constitute the cross, unless our sorrow is the result of a self-emptying in order that others may be served and somebody else may be saved."*

It is critical to remember both that we cannot die to self in the power of self and that we die to self so that others may live. Jesus is not a masochistic master calling us to deny self without reason or purpose. He is not into suffering and denial as goals in themselves, He merely teaches that they are necessary means for the saving of many lives. This is why Morgan also said: *"We have not touched the realm of the cross, when our suffering is peculiar to ourselves."* At its core, the crucified life is about others. And if we really love others we will live dead.

There is a joy in the crucified life if it is followed by resurrection power. But we don't get to resurrection power if we don't get to all the way dead. If we wriggle off our cross at 87% dead, we end up mutilated and scarred – but not resurrected. We get to all the way dead by not getting our way every day in multiple ways – and by coming to like it. When we are happy, genuinely happy for Jesus (first) and others to get their way early and often…we are well on our way to living the crucified life – to living dead – and to the resurrection power that surely follows. And only resurrection power can life the spiritually dead.

The crucified life consists not primarily in giving up bad things, but good ones. We give up good things for the glory of God among all nations. Jesus – the greatest Good – was given up for the saving of the nations. To follow Him to the cross requires the giving up of whatever is good for the same. Morgan puts it this way: "…*not that low things and vulgar things are to be given up, but that high and holy things and beautiful things, the most beautiful things of the world, the love of father, of mother, of wife, of child, of brother, and sister, and the love of life itself, if the hour shall ever strike when there is a conflict between loyalty to Him and these high loves, these are to be trampled underfoot.*"

In this excellent book, Dustin Renz lays out practical and biblical ways for us to live crucified – dead to self by the power of the Spirit that the resurrection power of Jesus may life others. The joy in living dead is that the same Spirit that raised Jesus from the dead will also life our mortal bodies so that pagans, Muslims, Buddhists, Hindus, Secular peoples, Animists… and friends and family may all find eternal life in Christ. Eternal life is the goal of the crucified life, self-denial is merely the path. The grand prize is life, eternal life. We just get there by dying.

Dick Brogden
Co-founder of the Live Dead Partnership
Assemblies of God World Missionary
UAE. November 2023.

"Some people have been misinformed about the Christian life and living the crucified life. For some reason, they think that it is an easy path. They believe that God will take away all of their problems and difficulties and that they will be able to live their lives without any kind of distraction or disturbance. As everybody who has traveled this journey knows, such is not the case. If your journey is not cluttered with difficulties and hardships and burdens, you just might be on the wrong path."

-A.W. Tozer[1]

"Jesus has many who love His Kingdom in Heaven, but few who bear His Cross. He has many who desire comfort, but few who desire suffering. He finds many to share His feast, but few His fasting. All desire to rejoice with Him, but few are willing to suffer for His sake. Many follow Jesus to the Breaking of Bread, but few to the drinking of the Cup of His Passion. Many admire His miracles, but few follow Him in the humiliation of His Cross."

-Thomas á Kempis[2]

"To be a follower of the Crucified means, sooner or later, a personal encounter with the Cross."

-Elisabeth Elliot[1]

# INTRODUCTION:

## A PRACTICAL PATH TO THE CROSS-CENTERED LIFE

WITH EVEN THE SLIGHTEST EXPOSURE to Christianity, I imagine anyone in the world would confidently identify a cross as the symbol most associated with the Christian faith. Two lifeless planks of wood nailed together carry no significance in and of themselves. However—for Christians—the symbol of the cross represents everything in which we have placed our hope. The Apostle Paul once wrote,

> For the message of the cross is foolishness to those who are perishing, but to us who are being saved it is the power of God.
> **(1 Corinthians 1:18)**

To the world, the emphasis we place on the cross is much ado about nothing. To the believer, the cross speaks volumes without saying a word.

It is representative of the very crux of our faith. But beyond its historical and symbolic significance, it is also important to ask how much impact the cross has on the daily life of the average believer. I suppose most of us have spent a substantial amount of time during our faith journey picturing our Savior hanging on the cross, dying the death that we deserve. However, very few of us have spent much time—if any at all—picturing ourselves there.

*It is time for that to change.*

For us to truly follow Jesus on His terms, the cross must be more than a mere symbol of our faith. It must become more to us than a piece of wood on which the Romans hung Jesus to die. The true power of the cross is in its invitation to take our self-lives and nail them to its crossbeam. The cross's power is activated when we intentionally choose to submit our lives to its authority and allow it to accomplish its work in our hearts today, in real-time.

This is what *The Crucified Lifestyle* is all about. Its message is for all followers of Jesus who have ever wrestled with their flesh and desire to find greater freedom. It is for those who have a yearning in their hearts for deeper intimacy with God but are not quite sure how to attain it. It is for the Christian who is honest enough to admit that the self-life continues to be an obstacle in serving God wholeheartedly. The cross-centered life is the answer for these and many other common struggles believers face. Applying the principles presented in the following pages can empower each of us to take tangible steps toward a more vibrant spiritual life.

*The Crucified Lifestyle* is not meant to provide an exhaustive study on the subject but rather to offer earnest readers practical guidance on how to conform their lives to the cross. The book is divided into four main sections, each examining the Crucified Lifestyle through a distinct lens. The first is the lens of definition, which describes Jesus' call to discipleship and explains how a crucifixion that took place two thousand years ago has practical application in the lives of His followers today. The second is the lens of victory, where we will identify three obstacles that every believer faces and discover how the Crucified Lifestyle empowers us to overcome each of them. The third lens is surrender where we will discuss three areas of our lives that must be fully submitted to the Lord as His disciples. The fourth and final lens is that of discipline. This section will discuss three practical spiritual disciplines that are crucial to our cross-centered journey.

Each of the nine principles in this book has been part of my own spiritual voyage with the Lord. I am simply one of Jesus' disciples who has endeavored to take up his cross to the best of my ability. Have I consistently embodied the principles in this book without fail? Not at all. My failures have been many and great. However, the Lord has continually been merciful by guiding me back onto the narrow path whenever I have strayed. I have discovered through personal experience that the abundant life is more than just a phrase from the Bible.[2] It is a tangible life available to all of God's adopted children. And it is the result of an exchange that takes place when we give our lives to Jesus and He, in turn, gives His life to us.

Join me as we embark on this journey together. I cannot promise it will be easy. There will be obstacles along the way. We will most certainly be challenged to get out of our comfort zones. But on the other side, it will be more than worth it. Let it be said of all of us reading these words that we took up our crosses, denied ourselves and followed Jesus.

# SECTION ONE:

## A CRUCIFIED LIFESTYLE

A few years ago, I was invited to speak at the Gospel Mission Bible School, located in the Netherlands, now in the town of Amerongen. While planning the trip, I had a discussion with their leadership about the speaking schedule. They advised me that one of my primary responsibilities was to present a twelve-session teaching to the full-time students who lived on campus. The theme was to be, "The Crucified Life."

Before beginning my research, I am certain I had a basic understanding of the topic. After all, having been a believer since the age of eighteen and in ministry for over ten years at that point, it could be assumed that a topic so fundamentally essential to our faith would be a familiar one. However, preparing those lessons forced me to spend much time in prayer and study about what the Bible had to say regarding the cross and the impact it should have in our lives. And what began as more of a textbook understanding of the Crucified Lifestyle has now become a central theme for my life.

This first section contains two chapters that lay a foundation for the remaining three sections of the book. To give a clear understanding of what is meant by the Crucified Lifestyle, it requires us to view it through the broadest lens of definition. The first chapter will introduce and answer the question, "What is the Crucified Lifestyle?" Chapter Two is titled, "The Path of Much Resistance," and will explain why the cross-centered life is such a challenge for believers to live out. Together, let us peer through the lens of definition to discover what it means to live the Crucified Lifestyle.

"Salvation comes through a cross and a crucified Christ."

-Andrew Murray[1]

## CHAPTER

# 1

## WHAT IS THE CRUCIFIED LIFESTYLE?

**IMAGINE WHAT IT WAS LIKE** to spend just one day with Jesus during His public ministry. His original disciples had nearly three consecutive years of such days. Out of the billions of people in the world's history, these twelve ordinary men had the unique privilege of walking with God in human form. Following Jesus must have been the most amazing adventure one could ever dream. At any time, someone could be radically healed, delivered of demons or a public debate could break out between Jesus and the Pharisees. No doubt, Christ must have had an air of excitement around Him during His public ministry.

Have you ever thought to yourself, "If only I could have been alive when Jesus walked the earth to see the miracles He performed first-hand, it would be so much easier to have faith"? I know that I have. However, when I picture myself as one of the original twelve disciples, it seems that following Jesus was probably a far more difficult task than we may presume. This is because Jesus operated in a way that was complicated. At times, people had difficulty getting a straight answer out of Him. Often, He would respond to a question with another question.[2] In other situations, He would share an obscure parable and then explain that He intentionally taught in mysteries so that people would not understand Him.[3] The disciples frequently pulled Jesus aside after the crowds had left to ask what He meant by His teachings because they were confused. But, perhaps the most challenging thing about following Christ would have been what He taught about the cost of discipleship.

A verse in Luke 9—which serves as the foundational text for this book—is one of these difficult teachings:

> If anyone desires to come after Me, let him deny himself, and take up his cross daily, and follow Me. (v. 23)

Let us look at the context of this verse to consider the events that had transpired in the lives of the disciples when Jesus first spoke these words to them.

## FEEDING THOUSANDS

Luke records a spectacular event in the ninth chapter of his Gospel account. Long story short, Jesus feeds a crowd of five thousand men (in addition to their wives and children) with just five loaves of bread and two fish. For those of us who grew up hearing this story, it may have lost its wonder. Perhaps a modern parallel would be helpful.

Let us suppose your church is holding an outreach and you are working the hot dog table. You realize you have five hot dogs left, and there are five hundred people in line. You look across the seemingly endless line of hungry faces and start planning your escape before the people realize that your church made a promise on which it could not deliver.

*Perfect time for a bathroom break.*

Now, think about what an amazing miracle it would be if you decided to stay the course and distribute the final hot dogs despite the impending disaster, but instead, you end up providing every person in line with enough food to be completely satisfied. Now multiply that miracle by at least twenty and you will get a glimpse of what took place that day in Jesus' ministry.

Can you picture the reaction of the disciples as they distributed the bread and fish to thousands without failing to feed a single person? This was just one example of what it was like to follow Jesus during His earthly ministry. The disciples must have felt like celebrities. They were the entourage and closest confidantes of the Miracle Worker Himself.

## THE MESSIAH HAS COME

Luke immediately transitions from that story to a discussion that Jesus had with His disciples. It began with Peter making the accurate declaration that Jesus was the "Christ of God." (vs. 20) With the amazing miracle of multiplication still fresh on his mind, Peter makes a definitive announcement about Jesus' identity. Without a proper understanding of the Jewish context around that phrase, "Christ of God," it might be difficult to grasp the significance of what Peter was expressing.

The word *Christ* in Greek is *Christos*, which means, "anointed"[4] and relates directly to the Hebrew word *mashiach*, from which the word *Messiah* is derived.[5] The Old Testament speaks about this anointed individual through multiple prophecies and provides many details about the deliverer for whom the Jewish people were to await. There were a few key characteristics that the Jews believed would be true about the coming Messiah. Two of the primary expectations were:

1. According to various passages in the Old Testament, the Messiah would be born from the line of King David. (II Samuel 7:12–16; Isaiah 11:1; Jeremiah 23:5–6)

2. The Messiah would also restore David's throne, making him a ruler. (Isaiah 9:7; Amos 9:11; Jeremiah 30:9; Ezekiel 37:24)

We can see how these expectations influenced King Herod's decisions in the events that transpired around the birth of Christ. Due to these predictions about the coming Messiah, Herod had all the children aged two and under put to death in an effort to protect his throne.[6] These Messianic prophecies were also evident in some of the comments that were recorded in the Gospels. For example, Jesus was often referred to as the "Son of David," a clear reference to the identity of the Messiah. Also in John 6, we read about Jesus having to escape a crowd whose plan was to take Him by force to make Him king. Due to His miracles, they drew the conclusion, "This is truly the Prophet who is to come into the world." (vs. 14-15)

The Jewish people envisioned that—one day—Jehovah would send a new ruler who would deliver them from their enemies and restore power to Israel. Groups like the Zealots were birthed out of the belief that Rome should be forcefully overthrown as a means of fulfilling the prophecies. Certainly, Jesus' gaining popularity would have seemed to indicate that He was going to become a powerful political ruler. You can hear this expectancy from Jesus' followers even after His resurrection from the dead. When He appeared to them before His ascension in Acts 1:6, they were still asking about His role in establishing the throne of David: "Lord, will You at this time restore the kingdom to Israel?" His followers were unable to understand how their interpretation of the Old Testament prophecies about the Messiah could mesh with Jesus' death, resurrection and ascension.

These expectations of the coming Messiah would have been on Peter's mind when he declared Jesus to be the Christ of God. In response, Jesus instructs the disciples to keep this revelation a secret. He then provides them with what must have seemed bizarre information at the time:

> The Son of Man must suffer many things and be rejected by the elders and chief priests and scribes, and be killed, and be raised up on the third day. (vs. 22)

Try to capture the scene that is unfolding here. The disciples had just played an active role in an event that resulted in over ten thousand people experiencing a miracle from their Rabbi. And they not only witnessed Jesus do the miracle, but they saw it take place through their own hands.

It must have seemed like they were on their way to the top. They probably whispered to each other, "This is it. It's what we've been waiting to see. Look at these crowds!"

It is in that atmosphere that Peter receives the revelation that Jesus is the Messiah and openly declares it. We do not know how Peter expected Jesus to respond. But instead of taking the time to expound upon Peter's epiphany, He immediately begins to describe suffering, rejection and death. Talk about putting a damper on an otherwise thrilling time of ministry!

I am certain that Peter, John and the other ten disciples must have been perplexed—and possibly even irritated—when Jesus started speaking this way. After all, these men were at the very epicenter of what was destined to become the greatest movement in history. They had been personally selected by the Messiah to follow Him as His disciples. As the crowds increased in size, they were looking to the future with great anticipation. They did not know how Jesus was going to accomplish it, but His popularity was soaring. Somehow, He would become a king and set up His earthly empire; it was just a matter of time.

From our perspective of the cross, the pain and suffering that Jesus was describing makes all the sense in the world. But can you imagine what was going through the minds of His disciples in that moment? At a time when they felt like they were ready to take on the world, why would their leader feel the need to talk about something so disconnected with their vision of the mission? When you read through the Gospels, you find that this was a typical experience for Jesus' followers. The ministry must have felt like taking one step forward and two steps back. But Jesus had a spiritual mission to fulfill which had an exceedingly greater significance than they could have understood at that time.

## THE HIGH COST OF DISCIPLESHIP

Attached to these foreboding words about His upcoming suffering and death, Jesus spoke our key text:

> If anyone desires to come after Me, let him deny himself, and take up his cross daily, and follow Me. **(Luke 9:23)**

I wonder what the disciples' facial expressions were when He spoke those words. Did Peter roll his eyes, wondering why Jesus refused to stick to a more upbeat advertising campaign? Were they bewildered, unable to comprehend how His words applied to them? We do not know for sure. All we have in the text are the red letters. However, regardless of *their* reaction, the text invites us to ask some questions of ourselves: What is the expression on *my* face when I consider Jesus' words? Am *I* offended at such a call? Am *I* confused? Do I believe this verse has any practical application in *my* life?

I think most of us assume that if we had been one of Jesus' original followers, we would have completely bought into everything He taught. We look at the disciples with an air of superiority, wondering why they just could not seem to grasp what Jesus tried to convey. We picture ourselves fully embracing His teachings without question. But there were times when the words that came out of our Savior's mouth sounded overly extreme, to put it lightly. And it is not just the original twelve disciples who stumbled over His difficult sayings, we are still tripping over them two thousand years later.

Jesus did not make discipleship sound like a joy ride. Modern-day teachings that present following Christ as a split-second decision made without considering its impact is a far cry from Jesus' description of the call. For example, in Luke 14, Jesus spoke these words to a large crowd of people:

> For which of you, intending to build a tower, does not sit down first and count the cost, whether he has enough to finish it—lest, after he has laid the foundation, and is not able to finish, all who see it begin to mock him, saying, 'This man began to build and was not able to finish'? Or what king, going to make war against another king, does not sit down first and consider whether he is able with ten thousand to meet him who comes against him with twenty thousand? Or else, while the other is still a great way off, he sends a delegation and asks conditions of peace. So likewise, whoever of you does not forsake all that he has cannot be My disciple. (**vss. 28-33**)

One thing is clear from Jesus' description of discipleship: there was a high price to be paid for those who would choose to follow Him. Discipleship was not for people who wanted to take the easy road, but for those who evaluated the cost and decided that He was worth it. It was not a, "raise your hand, pray this prayer and go back to your normal life" type of decision. It involved a complete shifting of priorities resulting in a radical life change. Discipleship was an all-in, no turning back commitment. As Walter Kaiser writes, "Repentance was not to be a halfhearted response to the gospel; it had to involve a major overhaul of a person's whole orientation to life."[7]

I fear this message has become unfashionable in many modern churches. The trend of today's sermons is often toward the blessings and benefits of following Christ. While these are both important and completely true, they are only one aspect of discipleship. How often do we share the message of Luke 9:23, "If you want to follow Jesus, you have to give up your life!" Instead, we tend to share the Gospel message in this manner:

> "If you want a better life…freedom from addiction…your marriage fixed…(fill in the blank)…accept Jesus as your Lord and Savior. If you do, He will forgive all your sins and you will go to Heaven."

We seldom discuss the cost of discipleship in the same terms that our Savior used. If Jesus Himself were to share His difficult sayings from our pulpits, some might criticize the message and say that it puts barriers between people and salvation. We are afraid if we told people the whole truth, no one would get saved. So, we become content with presenting a watered-down version of the Gospel and promising eternal life to people without communicating the very real cost that following Jesus demands. But who is better equipped to explain what it means to follow Christ, modern church-growth strategists or Jesus Himself? We do not set the rules and parameters of discipleship; He does.

The real challenge is not to determine what Jesus meant when He spoke about counting the cost, but whether we are willing to obey Him. He was not trying to discourage us from following Him. Rather, He was advising all who might consider discipleship that the cost was high, and the road would not always be easy.

## THE CROSS OF THE CRUCIFIED LIFESTYLE

The invitation that Jesus gave in Luke 9:23 included the requirement for each of His followers to, "take up his cross." The Greek word for *take up* is *airō* and means, "to take upon oneself and carry what has been raised, to bear."[8] In this case, Jesus is giving us a word picture that describes a disciple picking up a cross, placing it on his back and carrying it throughout his daily life. While it might seem to be an obvious foreshadowing of the way that Jesus was going to die, it is important to take into consideration that He spoke these words pre-crucifixion.

Think about the ramifications of that reality. When Jesus was sharing this truth, He had not yet hung upon a cross. There had been no resurrection or ascension, and the full plan of salvation had not been revealed to His disciples. Because of this, when Jesus' followers heard Him speaking about taking up a cross, their minds could not have imagined the beautiful cross of Christ that you and I would think about.

Our perception of the cross is much different in modern Christianity than it would have been to the first-century disciples. On this side of Calvary, the cross is the most beautiful symbol of God's love that humanity could ever know. In light of this, Christians have gone to great lengths to elevate the symbol of the cross. We make cross-shaped jewelry and decorations. We sing songs about it, such as the well-known hymn, The Old Rugged Cross. Our celebration of the cross is understandable. Through the death and resurrection of Christ, the cross has become the symbol of His complete victory over sin, hell and the grave. It is the sign of redemption and the hope of all mankind.

But while we rejoice in the cross, let us be very careful not to forget its original meaning. It is just as much an instrument of death when we hang it on a necklace as it was when Jesus informed His disciples that they would need to take one up themselves. If we only understand the cross from the vantage point of post-resurrection theology, it loses its intended jarring force. As A.W. Tozer once wrote:

> Its power departed when it was changed from a thing of death to a thing of beauty. When men made of it a symbol, hung it around their necks as an ornament or made its outline before their faces as a magic sign to ward off evil, then it became at best a weak emblem, at worst a [good luck charm]…We must do something about the cross, and one of two things only we can do—flee it or die upon it.[9]

Jesus spoke of taking up a cross to a group of followers who had no framework for the eternal significance of His coming death and resurrection. They were not thinking about a colorful, stained-glass scene in the window of a cathedral. They were not imagining Easter decorations or a cross graphic on a T-shirt. Their only framework for a cross would have been the instrument of torture and death that was reserved for criminals in the Roman Empire.\* Jesus' command in Luke 9 was meant to shock His audience considering what a cross represented during that period in history. It would be the equivalent of saying that anyone who wants to be His disciple must hang on the gallows, sit in the electric chair or take a lethal injection.

Perhaps now you can see the difference between the impact of Christ's words on His disciples and the average twenty-first century reader. They could not have thought that Jesus was referring to the abundant life they would enjoy after He gave Himself as a sacrifice for them. In their cultural context, they would have understood His message as a reference to some form of death that was required in order to follow Him. The amazing thing about the physical cross of Christ is that Jesus bore it once and for all in our place. He went to the *literal* cross so that we do not have to. But His willingness to take the cross upon Himself does not alleviate us from our calling to be cross-carriers. Let us further examine the *spiritual* meaning of Jesus' call to discipleship in Luke 9:23.

---

\*For more details on the crucifixion process of Jesus' day, see the Appendix (p. 219)

# THE REQUIREMENTS OF LUKE 9:23

Now that we have established the context around our foundational verse from Luke, we will briefly examine the phrases contained in the verse itself. Throughout the remainder of this book, each of these concepts will be broken down in much more detail.

*"If anyone desires to come after Me…"*

Jesus opens His call to discipleship by describing His target audience. He is communicating this truth specifically to those who want to become His disciples. With all the miracles, signs and wonders that He was performing—coupled with a growing understanding that He could be the long-awaited Messiah—it should come as no surprise that many would want to join His ranks. He then describes the lifestyle that is required of those people who desire to become one of His followers.

*"…let him deny himself…"*

Jesus goes on to say that His followers should deny themselves. The Greek word used is *arneomai*, which means, "to disregard one's own interests."[10] Those who follow Christ must be willing to set aside their own pursuits when discipleship demands it. This does not mean that His disciples cease having their own desires, or even that they will never be fulfilled. But, when they come into conflict with His desires, disciples must be willing to disregard their own for His sake. Douglas Petersen explains, "Jesus' call is not for ascetic self-denial but for disavowal of one's own desires in order for the kingdom of God to become the central focus of one's life."[11] Self-denial from a willing heart is a mark of true discipleship.

*"…and take up his cross daily…"*

As we have already discussed, this cross that Jesus is referencing is the equivalent of a death sentence. But what is the practical application of the requirement to take up a cross? Certainly, He could not have been referring to death on a physical cross. That form of capital punishment is not practiced in the world anymore. If that were the requirement, anyone who has lived after the fall of the Roman Empire would be disqualified, including you and me. In addition, even though most of His original followers were martyred for their faith—and some even on crosses—there were many who were not. Throughout the last two millennia, there have been countless followers of Christ who have died of natural causes. For these reasons, Jesus would not make physical death on a cross a requirement of discipleship.

While Jesus is referring to a form of death in this passage, it is not a physical death, but rather a spiritual death to self. Jesus was communicating the truth that the same intentional, forceful death of Roman crucifixion needs to be applied to the self-life of His followers. This is a spiritual discipline that every disciple must learn to truly walk with Christ. Notice He did not give any qualifying statements, such as, "If you want to be my *greatest* disciple, then you must take up your cross." Nor did He say, "If you want to be more intimate with me than my other disciples, take up your cross." He simply said *anyone* who wants to follow Him must take up a cross and carry it on a daily basis.

The cross is imperative for Jesus' followers. He was not giving us an option; He was giving us a requirement. The idea that someone can follow Christ and never die to themselves is contrary to His teaching. Jesus' call to discipleship is a mandatory death sentence to the self-life. In fact, in Matthew 10:38, Jesus tells us plainly, "He who does not take his cross and follow after Me is not worthy of Me."

### *"...and follow Me."*

The final requirement in this verse has to do with the concept of following. The word *follow* is *akoloutheō* in Greek, which can be defined in the context of discipleship as, "to cleave steadfastly to one, conform wholly to his example, in living and if need be, in dying also."[12] When Jesus spoke these words in Luke, He knew that He was headed to the cross of Calvary. Although the disciples did not understand what He was trying to convey, there would be suffering and death on the horizon. His disciples were to follow in His footsteps, even when it meant giving up their own lives.

Following someone else required that they forsook their own path, plans and pursuits, and instead made His leading their priority.

True discipleship is a much greater commitment than a profession of faith in a church service. For a person to "receive Christ" in a church, and then go back to the same lifestyle they lived before they went to church that day does not equate with following Jesus. Discipleship involves a change in the trajectory of one's life. It is a decision that will drastically alter the lives of Jesus' disciples.

## THE GOAL OF THE CRUCIFIED LIFESTYLE

Each of the requirements of Luke 9:23 affects the self-life of the disciple in a tangible way. When you consider what Jesus is expressing in His call to discipleship, it is a wonder that He had any followers at all. Even with the healings, deliverances, anointed teaching and miraculous provision, telling people that they would have to deny themselves, be crucified daily and upend their lives was sure to cause His potential followers to second-guess their decision. But why is the cross-centered life so important to the Lord? What is it about the self-life that makes God call for its crucifixion? The answer to that question can be found in the way that we were designed.

The Bible teaches us that God is love.[13] Selfless love is not just something He does; it is who He is. It is God's nature and desire to reveal that love to His creation. All humans are created in the image of God.[14] Because of this, we were designed and programmed to find true joy, not in living for ourselves, but in living for others as we reflect His love through our lives. The only reason that mankind is internally wired to live for self is because of sin's entrance into the human race. But when we learn to resist that natural selfish inclination and instead choose to live the selfless life of the cross, we will experience the most satisfying, joy-filled life imaginable. Love for others should be the natural outflow of a person who has truly died to their sinful nature and is living for the glory of God.

The commands of Christ cannot be obeyed unless we are willing to die to our own needs and desires. If we choose to follow Jesus, it demands that we embrace the commands of Scripture, such as:

- "Love one another." **(John 15:17)**
- "Be devoted to one another in love. Honor one another above yourselves." **(Romans 12:10 NIV)**
- "…not looking to your own interests but each of you to the interests of others." **(Philippians 2:4 NIV)**
- "…in humility value others above yourselves…" **(Philippians 2:3 NIV)**
- "Love your neighbor as yourself." **(Leviticus 19:18; Matthew 22:39)**

None of these commands can be fully obeyed unless we are willing to put our self-lives on a cross. We may find it difficult to accept this truth because it makes no sense to our natural minds and it is contrary to the way society teaches us to achieve happiness. However, those who have entered this lifestyle have found that true peace, joy and contentment are only found as we die to ourselves in order to pour the love of God into the lives of others. Jesus' call to discipleship is an invitation to live out the greatest life available to us on this earth!

# FINDING LIFE BY LOSING IT

The same One who spoke these words about taking up a cross also said He came that we may have life and have it more abundantly.[15] The question is where—and how—is that abundant life obtained? In Luke 9:24, Jesus goes on to say, "Whoever desires to save his life will lose it, but whoever loses his life for My sake will save it." This is the mystery of the Crucified Lifestyle. As we learn to die to ourselves, we find His life being lived in and through us. It is only through the crucifixion that His resurrection life can be manifested in our lives.

This important truth needs to be deeply embedded in our hearts. The Bible tells us that Jesus endured the cross "for the joy set before Him."[16] Our Savior set His eyes on the other side of the cross, which gave Him the strength and determination to undergo the suffering. His focus was on the end-result of what the Father was going to accomplish through His obedience. It is the same for us. We must look to the other side of losing our lives and focus on the joy of having His life more fully operable inside of us.

When we discuss the Crucified Lifestyle, the tendency is to think of all that we might have to give up to truly follow Christ. We are like the rich, young ruler who walked away disheartened because we do not want to surrender all.[17] What we should be considering is all that we gain! Sacrifice is involved, but deeper intimacy with the Lord is a treasure worth losing everything to achieve. A life surrendered to God is the most fulfilling life we could ever hope to experience. He is not asking us to pursue anything except for that which we *were already* designed to live. This is not a burdensome life; it is a joyous life. And for everything we give up, He gives back a hundredfold. As He says in Mark 10:

> Assuredly, I say to you, there is no one who has left house or brothers or sisters or father or mother or wife or children or lands, for My sake and the gospel's, who shall not receive a hundredfold now in this time—houses and brothers and sisters and mothers and children and lands, with persecutions—and in the age to come, eternal life. **(vss. 29-30)**

The blessings promised here are not only given to us in heaven but are available to us now! Let us keep our eyes focused on the joy set before us as we embrace the cross and surrender more fully to the Lord.

In this chapter, we have discussed the Crucified Lifestyle and the high cost of discipleship, including the denial, death and redirection of our self-lives. In the next chapter, we will discover why the Crucified Lifestyle is so often neglected—as well as resisted—in today's church culture.

"If you bear the cross unwillingly, you make it a burden, and load yourself more heavily; but you must needs bear it."

-Thomas a Kempis[1]

# CHAPTER

# 2

## THE PATH OF MUCH RESISTANCE

**P**ICTURE A MAN WHO LIVES in a region of the world where Christianity is non-existent. He has never heard the name of Jesus and knows nothing about the Bible. One day, this man finds a single page from the Gospels, which contains the ninth chapter of Luke. In his curiosity, he examines the teachings of Jesus carefully, especially what He communicates about the cost of becoming His disciple. He wonders if there are people in the world who still follow this Jesus that he is reading about.

What if he were to come to your hometown in search of the type of people whose lifestyle embodies what Luke's passage is describing? He would be looking for people who live in self-denial and have truly laid everything down in their pursuit of Jesus. If he attended your church, would he find Christians who are dying to themselves on a daily basis and following Christ on the terms He laid out in Luke 9:23? Or would he have difficulty finding people who are living the way that Jesus described?

It seems that the pathway of the Crucified Lifestyle is all too often untrodden by the feet of those who profess Christ in our society. There is plenty of space on the trail, but not enough willing to walk on it. The question we want to answer in this chapter is, "If Jesus said that His followers would deny themselves, take up their crosses and follow Him, why is there so much resistance to the Crucified Lifestyle?" As we discuss two primary obstacles to the cross-centered life, let us also search our own hearts for signs of resistance to Jesus' call.

## THE CULTURE BARRIER

The first major obstacle to the Crucified Lifestyle is culture, which can be defined as, "the characteristic features of everyday existence (such as diversions or a way of life) shared by people in a place or time."[2] The term *culture* includes the attitudes, values and goals shared by people in a given society. Each culture has its own unique set of rules and values that—whether for better or for worse—influence the standard of living, the driving force of people's lives and the overall spiritual atmosphere within it. James Plueddemann explains, "The worldview of a culture describes deep philosophical assumptions about the purpose of life and the nature of reality."[3]

Often people who are born and raised in a particular culture do not take time to consider the ideals that make their culture unique. We are like a fish who does not realize it is in water because life in the fishbowl is all it has ever known. Until we encounter a different culture, it is hard to identify what makes ours distinctive from others. If we take a step back and examine the culture of the West, we discover an increasingly secularized culture which places a high value on affluence, amassing possessions and the pursuit of personal comfort and happiness. Generally speaking, these are the priorities shared by the majority of people in Western society.

There is a self-centered drive for *more* and *better* that characterizes our culture. It is all about *me* and what I want. For instance, consider the advertising industry, which makes its fortunes by creating a sense of lack in its audience. The message that is communicated through advertisement is, "You need *this* to be satisfied in life." And many people in our society live with the nagging thought, "If I just had more of (blank), then I would be happy." Others think, "If I just had a better version of (blank), then happiness could be achieved." The message that our culture conveys to us is, "Life is all about you. Indulge yourself in every pleasure that your heart desires. After all, you only live once. Might as well enjoy it!"

This mentality creates a culture of people who are discontented and always pursuing something they believe they need to achieve happiness. Whatever version of satisfaction people are searching for, it is always elusive. They get a taste of it, and it leaves them longing for more. They get the expensive car they wanted and then notice someone else with a more luxurious one. They achieve some desired experience, but it does not satisfy the way they had hoped it would. They never obtain a sense of true fulfillment because the things of this world were never designed to provide that for people.

## A CULTURED CHURCH

Christians are not immune from culture's lure. Every generation of the church has existed within the framework of a worldly culture. While culture looks different in other parts of the world and time periods in history, believers have always had to contend with aspects of culture that can become a stumbling block to the cross-centered life. The unbiblical values of any given culture should not be a force of influence inside the church. In fact, the opposite should be true. The church should be influencing the culture around it with the values of God's Kingdom. Unfortunately, in Western society, oftentimes we see the dominant culture creeping into the church at an alarming rate. Believers who endeavor to live the Crucified Lifestyle will at times find themselves swimming against, not only the culture of the world, but even the culture of the worldly church around them.

The pursuit of wealth and worldly pleasure can be clearly seen in the lives of many professing Christians. If we are honest, we would have to admit that many of us have adopted these values and share them in common with people who have no relationship with God. When it comes to lifestyle and pursuit, the line between the church and the world has become immensely blurred. Although we may have some theological beliefs about Jesus' call to discipleship, when it comes to applying it practically, there is often a great disparity between our lives and our professed beliefs. It could be said that we often choose a Cultured Lifestyle rather than a Crucified one. We would be wise to ask ourselves, "Have I allowed the culture around me to have more influence in my life than the principles of God's Kingdom?"

## THE PARADOX OF THE KINGDOM OF GOD

The reason that Western culture is such an obstacle to the Crucified Lifestyle is that its core values are completely contradictory to the values of the Kingdom of God. The spiritual principles that govern His Kingdom are impossible to understand from a human-centered perspective. This incongruence is best defined with the term *paradox*, which is "a seemingly absurd or contradictory statement, even if well-founded."[4] An example of paradoxical spiritual laws can be found in the following passages:

- If anyone desires to be first, he shall be last of all and servant of all. (**Mark 9:35**)

- Whoever desires to become great among you shall be your servant. (**Mark 10:43**)

- For everyone who exalts himself will be humbled, and he who humbles himself will be exalted. (**Luke 18:14**)

- For whoever desires to save his life will lose it, but whoever loses his life for My sake will save it. (**Luke 9:24**)

- For when I am weak, then I am strong. (**2 Corinthians 12:10**)

- Therefore humble yourselves under the mighty hand of God, that He may exalt you in due time. **(1 Peter 5:6)**

None of these spiritual truths can be understood by human reasoning. They sound like foolishness to those who have been trained by the philosophies of our culture. Yet, in God's Kingdom, this is the normal way everything operates. It is impossible to embrace these spiritual realities without the illumination of the Holy Spirit. And even to those who have been reborn, these principles are still contradictory to our natural understanding. They need to be embraced by faith, even when they cannot be explained intellectually. Our problem is not a lack of information, but a lack of application. We need to choose which kingdom we want to live for, either the Kingdom of God or the kingdom of this world.

The value systems of these two kingdoms are in strong opposition to each other on many fronts. While our culture tells us, "The purpose of life is to acquire as much money and possessions as you can," Jesus says, "Life does not consist in the abundance of the things [we] possess."[5] When culture says, "It's all about you and your happiness. Do whatever you can to please yourself," Jesus says, "You must deny yourself and take up your cross daily and follow me."[6] If we follow Christ on His terms, we will often find ourselves living the complete opposite lifestyle of those who are following the world's values, both inside and outside of the church.

The cross of the Crucified Lifestyle does not make sense to a world that has no value for self-denial. It is ludicrous to those who choose to pursue comfort and happiness rather than live according to Scripture. But prioritizing the values of Western culture actually prevents the very life that it promises to its constituents. Selfish living leads to deeper bondage while selfless living leads to a more fulfilled life. The principles of our culture require a person to get off the cross to try to find abundant life in places where it simply does not exist.

# THE MAIN SOURCE OF RESISTANCE

While the external culture around us is a significant barrier to the

Crucified Lifestyle, there is another primary obstacle to the cross-centered life. The greatest battle we face is an internal force called the human will. *Will* is defined as, "the faculty by which a person decides on and initiates action."[7] Our will is a component of our soul, which also includes our intellect and emotions, and is the chief opponent of the practice of self-denial.

For most Christians, the problem is not a lack of knowledge about what Jesus taught in the Gospels. Many could probably quote Luke 9:23 from memory: "If anyone desires to come after Me, let him deny himself, and take up his cross daily, and follow Me." We see the lifestyle of self-denial that Jesus and His followers in the New Testament modeled for us. The issue is in our willingness. When it comes down to the question, "Am I personally willing to live the Crucified Lifestyle?" the answer is not always a resounding "Yes."

Some professing Christians are only willing to follow Jesus when it does not cost them anything. We see this resistance to full surrender by the followers of Jesus in John 6. Great multitudes wanted to follow Him because they saw the miracles He was performing. But when their level of commitment was challenged by His teaching, they said, "This is a hard saying; who can understand it?" A few verses later, John records, "From that time many of His disciples went back and walked with Him no more."(vs. 66) These followers from John 6 physically walked away when they realized that discipleship would require great sacrifice. The Lord's will did not line up with theirs, so they made the decision to stop following Him completely.

In the modern church, rejecting God's will does not always look so cut and dry. For the professing Christian in today's church who does not want to obey Jesus wholeheartedly, there is a temptation to follow Him under pretense rather than walking completely away. Some choose to continue displaying outward signs of obedience, while denying Him a fully surrendered life. They might recite the right platitudes and portray a Christian life, but in their hearts, they have drawn a line that they are unwilling to cross. Whether a professing Christian chooses to completely walk away, or to stay in church and put up a religious front, the resistance stems from the same source: the human will.

# THE HUMAN WILL

In defining the human will and why it exists, it is necessary to understand what it means for humans to be created in the image of God. The phrase "image of God" can be found in the Bible as early as Genesis 1:27, "So God created man in His own image; in the image of God He created him; male and female He created them." The image of God encompasses several characteristics that humans share with their Creator. When God created mankind, He made us distinct from all other creatures. Although we are not deities, we share many of His attributes. These include our ability to reason and make decisions, experience emotion and exercise our free will.

The capacity to choose how we will live, and conversely how we choose not to live, is a process that occurs both individually and internally. How we carry out those decisions is directly related to our motives. The Lord created us to use our free will to love, serve and obey Him. However, the default programming of the sinful nature is to make decisions based on what causes our greatest benefit and prevents the most pain. Self-serving and self-preservation have become the typical mode of operation for humans.

God created humans with a free will despite the possibility that men and women would exercise that will to reject Him. In the Garden of Eden, that risk turned into reality when Adam and Eve decided to eat of the Tree of the Knowledge of Good and Evil, which the Lord had clearly forbidden them to eat.[8] This is the first instance of humans deliberately rejecting God's will for the sake of their own, a rebellion that has played out countless billions of times in human history.

Knowing that humans could and would sin, why would God give us free will in the first place? Have you ever considered the fact that God planted the Tree of the Knowledge of Good and Evil? He intentionally provided Adam and Eve with the opportunity for temptation. Genesis 2:9 says that the tree was in the midst of the Garden. Why would He plant a forbidden tree right in plain view, knowing that Adam and Eve would have the choice to sin?

The answer is simple, yet profound: If people had no capacity to choose to sin, they would not have the ability to lovingly obey God. From the beginning, the Lord created us for relationship. His desire was to have people whom He could love and who would love Him in return. Philip Steyne explains:

> Men and women were endowed with the ability to choose between good and evil, to respond positively or negatively, to God's offer of fellowship. God risked creating such a creature because He wanted part of His creation to have a meaningful, purposeful relationship with Himself.[9]

If God had made a creature that had no choice but to love Him, could it truly love? Imagine you have the skills to design and build a robot. You program it to have its own unique personality and cause it to function the way you desire. Suppose you design it to behave as a close friend and program it to continuously compliment you. Would you honestly believe anything that the robot was expressing? A robot has no thinking of its own. It cannot experience emotion. It makes no decisions. It simply does what it is programmed to do. Therefore, only a person in delusion would accept the robot's words as a genuine compliment. And this would be a perfect picture of the type of creatures we would be if the Lord had not designed us with free will. It is impossible to have true relationship with pre-programmed creatures. So, if creating the human race was all about seeking genuine relationship with God, free will was a necessary component of our design.

The Lord's intention for humans was always for us to live in submission to His will. Had we done that from the beginning, we would still be living in paradise. However, sin caused mankind to live according to our own individual volition and reject the Lord's desire for our lives. Though some would say that the first sin in the Garden occurred the moment Adam and Eve sunk their teeth into the fruit of the tree, the sin actually took place when they purposed in their hearts to use their free will to reject God's command. Before a bite of flesh was removed from the fruit, sin had already entered humanity. And every tragedy in the world since that time can be traced back to that one rebellious decision. The will that God purposed to be a great blessing became the source of great tragedy.

## THE HUMAN CONDITION

Adam and Eve were created perfect; in a sinless state. However, their decision to rebel against God introduced sin into the world, and every person after has been born with a sinful nature. People are still created in God's image, but that image has been marred because of sin. Rather than having an innate desire to obey and please our Creator, mankind's chief concern became pleasing and protecting ourselves. The goal of our existence changed from living for God's glory to living for self. Sin caused us to become rebels against the Lord. And even as Christians, we still need to grapple with our desire to live selfishly. Our self-ambition is not automatically eradicated when we are born again. Rather, we must develop the discipline of dying to our sinful nature so that we can live for the will of God.

The fact of the matter is that most of us do everything we can to avoid pain and discomfort. We want a happy life, free from suffering and sorrow. Yet, following Jesus demands that we die to ourselves, which can be both uncomfortable and painful. There are many spiritual activities in the Christian life that our flesh will resist. If it were not for the Holy Spirit inside of us, we would have no desire to pray, fast or share our faith with others. Our spirits long to participate in the disciplines of the faith because they bring glory to God and draw us closer to Him. But in the natural, these practices are not something we would pursue on our own. As Jesus said, "The spirit indeed is willing, but the flesh is weak."[10]

## JESUS' HUMAN WILL

It is interesting to note that even Jesus had a free will that needed to be submitted to God's. Even though He was fully deity, He was born into the human race and became one of us.[11] In Matthew 26, Jesus cried out to God in the Garden of Gethsemane. He asked His Father to allow the cup of suffering to pass from Him. He made His request three times, and apparently the Father's answer was "No," based on the progression of events that followed. Jesus closed His prayer with the phrase, "Not as I will, but as You will."[12]

This passage reveals to us that Jesus was born with His own, individual human will. Jesus did not want to suffer the physical, spiritual, emotional or mental anguish of the cross. And yet, He knew the Father's will was that He die for humanity. And Philippians 2:8 tells us that, "being found in appearance as a man, He humbled Himself and became obedient to the point of death, even the death of the cross." Jesus submitted His will to God's will and chose to obey, even at the cost of His own life.

It was necessary for Jesus to have His own will on the earth, or He would not truly have been one of us. The temptation in the wilderness was meaningless if Jesus could not have chosen what Satan was offering.[13] Temptation cannot exist without free will. Without a will, Jesus would have been like a pre-programmed robot, and the writer of Hebrews could not have written, "For we do not have a High Priest who cannot sympathize with our weaknesses, but was in all points tempted as we are, yet without sin."[14] Like you and I, Jesus also had a free will of His own. Yet, He showed us it was possible to live a life of full submission to God.

## A LIFE OF SUBMISSION

Throughout the Gospels, we discover that Jesus chose to live in perfect submission to the will of His Father. In fact, He never stepped outside of God's will, even when His faithfulness caused Him to experience rejection, scorn, mockery and unbelief from people in His life. Jesus set the example of what it looks like to do the will of God in every situation. Obviously, you and I will not live perfectly submitted lives. But those who live the Crucified Lifestyle will strive to obey the will of God even when it clashes with our own.

Most believers are content in doing the Lord's will when it falls in line with what we already desire. If He asked us to walk up a steep hill in the dead of winter to seek out a man who would give us a backpack full of cash at the top, we would gladly obey. Even with the suffering involved in climbing a hill in frigid temperatures, the end result would motivate us to willingly submit to the Lord's will.

However, when Jesus tells us to deny ourselves, give our money away, go on a fast, or share the Gospel with our neighbor, suddenly we have every excuse to resist. As Christians, we can talk ourselves out of almost anything that is inconvenient or uncomfortable. This is because we are experiencing the clash of two wills. And the true litmus test of submission to God's will is found in our obedience in the areas that we are not naturally inclined to obey.

Submission to God involves a character trait called meekness, which can be defined as, "the willing submission of one person to the will of another."[15] When we willingly choose to do what the Lord asks despite our own desires or inclinations, we are displaying an attitude of meekness. Submission involves more than having knowledge of the Scriptures or God's will for our lives. It is actually *doing* whatever He asks, regardless of the personal cost. Anyone can claim to love Jesus, but He said, "If you love me, keep My commandments."[16] Walking meekly before God in obedience to His will is evidence of a truly Crucified Lifestyle.

## AN EASY YOKE

Jesus made the following statement in the book of Matthew:

Come to Me, all you who labor and are heavy laden, and I will give you rest. Take My yoke upon you and learn from Me, for I am gentle and lowly in heart, and you will find rest for your souls. For My yoke is easy and My burden is light. **(Matthew 11:28-30)**

The illustration used in this passage comes from first century farming. The Greek word for *yoke* is *zygos*, which is a wooden bar that is placed over the necks of two oxen to help them pull a load together.[17] In Jesus' time, in order to train a younger, inexperienced ox, sometimes a farmer would yoke it together with a more mature one. By working in tandem with the older ox, the younger ox could avoid bearing the brunt of the burden because the stronger ox would shoulder the majority of the weight, while at the same time guiding the path for both oxen. However, if the young ox decided it wanted to go its own way, the wooden yoke would restrain him and make it very difficult to break away from the path that the older ox was taking.

Jesus uses this example to describe our relationship with Him. His yoke is easy when we are walking according to His ways and with the guidance of His Spirit. But living out our faith becomes an arduous struggle when we are unwilling to fully surrender. Some view the concept of losing their lives for Christ's sake as something to be resisted rather than embraced. However, being yoked with the Lord is meant to be a blessing to us. The more we submit to His leadership, the more fulfilling and fruitful our discipleship journey will become.

## ARE WE WILLING?

Our willingness to embrace the cross becomes increasingly challenging when the personal cost is greater. What if following Jesus meant experiencing rejection from our closest friends? What if it meant being cast out of our families? What if discipleship cost us our reputations, our careers or even our lives? In some cultures, these risks are a reality. Many who choose to follow Christ in dangerous circumstances know in advance that it could cost them everything. Some are dying for their faith even as these words are being written.

Although there may be some consequences for following Jesus in the Western world, as of right now, they are typically not as drastic as these examples. But the question is not whether we will personally face these scenarios, but are we *willing*? What if we knew that it would cost everything to follow Jesus? Would we still submit to His will? Or would we shrink back and walk away like many have over the last two millennia?

Many Christians believe they would not deny Jesus if someone tried to force them at gunpoint. However, that is a hypothetical situation that will never become reality for most of us. The real question is whether we are denying Him in our daily lives. Do we deny Him in our workplaces? Do we deny Him in our schools? Are we living out our faith openly and sincerely, or are we holding back for fear of what others might think of us?

What we often discover in our churches are people who want the blessings of following Christ, without the willingness to embrace the cross. People want the Lord to move in their midst, but they do not want to sacrifice for it. They want God to bless them, but they are not willing to deny themselves. Essentially, they want the resurrection power without the crucifixion. But resurrection life does not come except through the cross.

We need to consider our level of willingness to follow Jesus on His terms. The Crucified Lifestyle may seem like an uphill battle when you consider the forces that are opposing us. To deny ourselves requires that we walk in a way contrary to the culture that surrounds us. It involves a level of discipline and intentionality that may not be commonplace among our Christian friends. It necessitates that we learn to submit our free will to the Lord and follow Him regardless of the personal cost.

As we take the time to evaluate our own level of commitment to the principles of Luke 9:23, we will now transition into the next section of the book. In the following three chapters, we are going to examine three realities of the Crucified Lifestyle that are life-transformative for those who choose to live them out.

# SECTION TWO:

## A VICTORIOUS LIFESTYLE

Now that we have examined the Crucified Lifestyle through the broad lens of definition, in this section, we are going to view it through the lens of victory. Through our union with Jesus in His death and resurrection, all believers are invited into a lifestyle of astounding spiritual triumph. However, our cooperation and determination are required to enjoy the fullness of the victorious life that God intends for us.

The term *victory* is defined as, "the process of defeating an enemy in battle or war or an opponent in a contest."[1] Each of the three practical principles in this section reflect forces that every believer will have to contend with as they endeavor to live the Crucified Lifestyle. These forces—sin, the world and the opinions of other people—have already been overcome by Jesus through His sacrifice. The battle was decided at the cross, and the victory has been made available to each of us. We decide for ourselves if we will walk in the victory provided or allow these forces to continue to have power over our lives. How we choose to engage with these principles will determine whether our lives will be characterized by triumph or defeat.

In the following chapters, we will discover three incredible benefits made available to every believer as a result of our participation in Christ's crucifixion.

"If you will not have death unto sin, you shall have sin unto death! There is no alternative; if you do not die to sin, you shall die for sin, and if you do not slay sin, sin will slay you!"

-Charles Spurgeon[1]

CHAPTER

3

## CRUCIFIED TO SIN

*Crucified Christians are Free from Sin's Power*

THE PROPENSITY TO SIN IS a universal trait shared among all people since the Fall. It is this unfortunate condition that puts us all on the same spiritual plane. This is why Romans 3:23 asserts, "For all have sinned and fall short of the glory of God." Regardless of social status, financial position or political power, every one of us has a sinful nature that longs for that which God forbids. As the saying goes, "The ground is level at the foot of the cross."

Have you ever wondered what it would be like to live in a sinless state? Adam and Eve had that opportunity. In fact, they were not only sinless at creation, but they inhabited a world that had not yet been cursed with sin. Jesus also lived in a sinless state, yet in a world where sin had already taken its toll. However, the rest of us have only experienced life with a sinful nature in a sin-stricken world. The Bible speaks to us about a place untainted by sin that will be the eternal reward for God's children.[2] For those born into this broken world, a sinless existence seems more the setting of a fairy tale than a possibility. We have been so affected and infected by sin, to imagine a world without it is almost impossible. Due to its enormous impact on the human race, it should come as no surprise that the concept of sin is one of the most frequently discussed topics in the Bible.

## THE BELIEVER'S RELATIONSHIP WITH SIN

The Apostle Paul spoke often in his epistles about the relationship between sin and God's children. In Romans 6:6, he tells us:

> …knowing this, that our old man was crucified with Him, that the body of sin might be done away with, that we should no longer be slaves of sin.

What Paul is expressing in this verse is not poetic filler. The Holy Spirit led him to write these words to reveal a powerful truth to the church. We discover in this verse that the Crucified Lifestyle is one that is free from the power of sin.

This is a tremendous blessing afforded to us by the cross. Scripture is plain that we were fully under the power of sin before we came to Christ. Paul writes in Romans 3:9, "For we have already made the charge that Jews and Gentiles alike are all under the power of sin." (NIV) And in Galatians 3:22, "But the Scriptures declare that we are all prisoners of sin…" (NLT) The Scriptures and our own experience teach us that sin was our master before Christ. We did what sin told us to do and were unable to do anything else. We lived for sin and self and were essentially captives in a prison of rebellion against God. But everything changed at the cross. Sin lost its power over us.

However, due to the continued presence of sin in the lives of professing Christians, this important theological truth is one that has been questioned. We live in a time when sin is increasingly practiced and accepted among those who claim to follow Jesus. Yet, we are warned in Jude 4 that ungodly people will secretly slip into the church and change the message of God's grace into an excuse—or license—to sin. If ever there was a time when we see that happening in the Body of Christ, it is now.

There is a message gaining popularity today that attempts to redefine grace. It teaches that, because grace covers all our sin, we are free to live as we please. Rather than seeing sin as a cancer for our souls and dealing with it accordingly, sin is seen as a small scrape to which we need only apply the Band-Aid of grace and not be concerned if the bleeding does not stop. But what relationship should believers expect to have with sin? The church's perspective on how to answer that question varies.

On one side, sin is seen as an expected and continuous aspect of our lives, and therefore its presence is not too alarming. "After all," some will say, "we are only human." Yet, on the opposite end of the spectrum, some teach that every time a believer sins, they should fear the judgment of hell. Certainly, the Bible must provide answers about an issue that has such an impact on how we live. In order to bring light to that discussion, I want to look at a theologically rich portion of Scripture: Romans 6-8. We will work through some of the key passages in these chapters to gain an understanding of the relationship that born again believers are supposed to have with sin according to the Bible.

# DEAD TO SIN

In Romans 5, Paul declares that grace comes because of sin. In the first verse of chapter 6, Paul raises the question that may logically follow this train of thought, "Shall we continue in sin that grace may abound?" One might suppose that in order to have more grace, why not sin more? But Paul insists that the answer to that question is, "No!" Then he tells us why: "How shall we who died to sin live any longer in it?" (vs. 2)

Notice that Paul is using the past tense to describe this death to sin. When did we die to sin's power? Again, verse 6 tells us plainly, "Our old man was crucified with Him, that the body of sin might be done away with, that we should no longer be slaves of sin." Here, the Scriptures inform us that our old self was crucified with Jesus on the cross. This happened at salvation, when we came to faith in Christ and He gave us His Holy Spirit as a deposit.³ At conversion, we were united with Christ in His crucifixion. (vs. 5) This union with Christ in His death is a spiritual reality for all born again believers.

Paul refers to a believer's death to sin as a finished work. He uses emphatic language to describe our new relationship with sin, saying we are "dead to sin," no longer "slaves of sin" and "freed from sin." These descriptive phrases are supposed to draw a clear distinction between us and the sin to which we were once entangled before salvation. Paul's words are meant to create a mental picture of distance, as if a great chasm is separating us from sin.

The passage then explains that Jesus was the first to die to sin (vs. 10), and because of our union with Him, we are also encouraged to count—or reckon—ourselves, "to be dead indeed to sin, but alive to God in Christ Jesus our Lord." (vs. 11) When Paul uses the term *reckon*, he is using a mathematical term that means, "to compute, calculate, take into account, determine."⁴ Anyone who has become one with Christ in His death can logically conclude that they are dead to sin, just like Him.

Paul then gives us a clear command: "Therefore do not let sin reign in your mortal body, that you should obey it in its lusts." (vs. 12) Here, Scripture tells us that we have a responsibility in light of these truths, which is to prevent sin from reigning in our lives. If sin is ruling in any area, it is because we have allowed it to against God's will. Paul tells us, "Sin shall not have dominion over you." He goes on to explain that, even though we were once slaves to sin, we are now under grace. (vs. 14) Anyone who examines these verses can see that Paul is making a strong argument that sin is not acceptable in the life of a Christian. Sin is incongruent to the Crucified Lifestyle.

## WHO IS OUR MASTER?

In the next section, Paul expounds on the illustration of slavery. He tells us,

> But God be thanked that though you were slaves of sin, yet you obeyed from the heart that form of doctrine to which you were delivered. And having been set free from sin, you became slaves of righteousness. **(vss. 17-18)**

Paul uses the system of slavery that was common in his culture as a natural illustration of a spiritual reality. He is referring to a change of life-ownership. We used to be slaves to sin. However, because of Jesus' death and resurrection, we are now slaves of righteousness. The loyalty that we once had to sin has now been redirected to righteousness as children of the King.

Paul advises us that this change of ownership should make a practical difference in our lives. Verse 22 says, "The benefit you reap leads to holiness, and the result is eternal life." (NIV) Because we no longer belong to sin, we should bear different fruit in our lives as evidence that we serve a new master. Holiness should now be characteristic of our lifestyle because our allegiance to sin has been severed by the cross.

# THE BELIEVER'S RELATIONSHIP WITH THE LAW

As we move into the beginning of Romans 7, Paul transitions the conversation from our death to sin resulting from our spiritual crucifixion, to our death to the Law. Paul's background provides us with context about what he is trying to express to his readers. As a Jew and former Pharisee, Paul was a man who had spent much of his life before salvation trying to obey the Old Covenant Law. Before his encounter with Jesus on the road to Damascus,[5] he was known as Saul of Tarsus, the zealous Pharisee, whose identity was completely wrapped up in legalistic righteousness.

Saul was born into a Jewish family and was also a Roman citizen. He had studied the Hebrew Scriptures under the well-respected rabbi, Gamaliel.[6] As part of his Pharisaic training, he would have been expected to study, memorize and interpret large portions of the Torah (the first five books of the Bible) as well as many other Scriptures. Saul makes his appearance in the book of Acts as a fierce persecutor of the Christian church. He was present during the stoning of Stephen, the first Christian martyr,[7] and worked diligently to arrest both male and female Christians.[8] In fact, in Acts 9, he was on his way to Damascus with the specific intent of arresting believers and destroying the Christian community.

Saul had dedicated his life to the Jewish faith and was a devout Pharisee. In his own words, he was:

> Circumcised on the eighth day, of the people of Israel, of the tribe of Benjamin, a Hebrew of Hebrews; in regard to the law, a Pharisee; as for zeal, persecuting the church; as for righteousness based on the law, faultless. (**Philippians 3:5-6 NIV**)

To claim that his righteousness was faultless is a bold statement. He obviously took obedience to the Law very seriously. And this is why many of his epistles speak about the role of the Law in a believer's life. Any Christian who had been saved out of Judaism would have had many concerns about what role the Old Testament Law was to play in their new walk of faith. This topic was of particular significance to the early church for this reason.

Paul uses the analogy of marriage to illustrate this principle. If a woman is married to a man, the Law required that she stay faithful to him. The only way that the Law would release her from that responsibility is if her husband were to die. Paul says:

> Therefore, my brethren, you also have become dead to the law through the body of Christ, that you may be married to another— to Him who was raised from the dead, that we should bear fruit to God. (**Romans 7:4**)

Essentially, Paul is informing us that our union with Christ's death releases us from the demands of the Old Covenant Law. And as Paul explains, this is "so that we should serve in the newness of the Spirit and not in the oldness of the letter." (vs. 6) Paul is not saying we are free from obeying God's moral instruction. That would contradict what he said about not sinning so that grace might increase. Instead, he is describing a life in which we live according to the Holy Spirit, who will not lead us in a way that is contrary to God's moral expectations. At this point in Paul's letter, the conversation is fairly straightforward. We are not only dead to sin as Crucified Christians, but also dead to the Law.

## THE LAW'S RELATIONSHIP WITH SIN

Now that Paul has established that believers are dead to the Law, he goes on to explain the relationship between the Law and sin. This theme is common in the Pauline epistles. Frequently in his letters, Paul makes it clear that the primary purpose of the Old Covenant was to help us to see our sin rather than to make us righteous. Romans 3:20 states, "Therefore no one will be declared righteous in God's sight by the works of the law; rather, through the law we become conscious of our sin." (NIV)

When God gave Israel the Law, His chief purpose was to show them that they could not keep it. The message of the Old Testament is that sinful people cannot be good enough to earn their righteousness in the eyes of a holy God. In Romans 7:7-13, Paul makes a compelling argument about this truth. He explains that the Law reveals the presence and power of sin to us. And Paul shows how this took place in his own life, by using covetousness as an example. He tells us that sin took the opportunity that the Law provided to produce in him "all manner of evil desire." (vs. 8) Paul explains, "For sin, taking occasion by the commandment, deceived me, and by it killed me." (vs. 11) It may seem like the Law is to blame for sin, but in actuality, the boundaries defined by the Law reveal our own sinful desires when we are tempted to cross them. Walter Kaiser explains, "The law develops our sense of sin when we see ourselves over against that to which God has called us."[9] Paul assures his readers that the Law is not sinful, but holy, just and good. (vs. 12) It teaches us about sin so that we will experience conviction when we break God's commandments. There is no issue with the Law of God; the problem is with the sinful hearts of men.

I do not believe that there can be much theological debate about what Paul has written up to this point in Romans. He has set before us some basic theological truths about sin, salvation and the Law that are not difficult to understand. While they may be challenging to put into practice in our lives, they are not complex concepts.

## A CONTROVERSIAL PASSAGE

Now we come to a very challenging portion of Scripture. In fact, the second half of Romans 7 is a hotbed of controversy in the theological world. The reason for the difficulty is that when you get to verse 14, the tone of Paul's letter completely changes. He writes: "We know that the law is spiritual, but I am unspiritual, sold as a slave to sin." (NIV) If you read this verse in context with everything that Paul has been trying to express to his audience, you get a conflicting message. Paul already established that we are dead to sin and no longer slaves to it. Now, he seems to be claiming that the opposite is true. He then goes on to describe a life of slavery to sin in the following verses:

> For what I am doing, I do not understand. For what I will to do, that I do not practice; but what I hate, that I do. If, then, I do what I will not to do, I agree with the law that it is good. But now, it is no longer I who do it, but sin that dwells in me. For I know that in me (that is, in my flesh) nothing good dwells; for to will is present with me, but how to perform what is good I do not find. For the good that I will to do, I do not do; but the evil I will not to do, that I practice. Now if I do what I will not to do, it is no longer I who do it, but sin that dwells in me. (vss. 15-20)

These verses describe a spiritual struggle in which Paul seems unable to do the good things that he desires, and instead, practices the evil that he does not want to do. The overall tone of this section is one of helplessness and hopelessness. Because of this, scholars have been debating this passage for centuries to try to identify the person to whom Paul is referring. There is no doubt that he is describing a battle against sin in this passage. But who is he trying to illustrate in this first-person narrative?

## WHO IS THE ROMANS 7 MAN?

In response to the confusion about this passage, scholars have formed divided opinions over whether Paul is referring to a battle with sin before or after salvation. A compelling argument can be made for both positions. In fact, there are several variations that fall under two main schools of thought. For our purposes, we will briefly examine these two possibilities in the broadest sense.

The first potential interpretation is that Paul is trying to describe a true believer's struggle against sin. Proponents of this argument point to Paul's statement in verse 22 about, "delighting in the law of God," as evidence that he was talking about himself after his conversion. The argument is that an unsaved person would not speak about himself in these terms. This perspective teaches that Paul is attempting to describe the battle between his two natures and the intense struggle that came as a result of it. He seems to allude to this in verse 25, "I myself in my mind am a slave to God's law, but in my sinful nature am a slave to the law of sin." (NIV) There are differing opinions about the spiritual maturity of the Christian Paul is describing, whether he is referring to a mature or immature believer. But those who adopt this position state that Paul is speaking from a post-salvation perspective.

The biggest objection to this viewpoint is that it sounds like Paul is confessing to a life defeated by sin. It is as if he is saying, "I know what I said in Romans 6 about being dead to sin, but when it comes to my everyday life, that is just not a reality." It seems Paul is speaking about sin as an enemy that is too powerful to overcome. All of us who have struggled with sin can certainly find common ground with Paul in Romans 7. We can relate to the frustration of trying not to sin and yet sometimes caving to temptation. While there is no doubt that we are susceptible to it, Paul has already informed us to reckon ourselves dead to sin and refuse to let it reign in our bodies. So, even if Paul is trying to describe a believer's struggle with sin, he has already explained how to deal with it as those who have been united with Jesus in His crucifixion.

If Paul is speaking about a believer's struggle with sin, the contradictory nature of this passage could be explained by concluding that this portion of his letter is a digression from describing the Crucified Lifestyle in Romans 6. This may be Paul's attempt to show what life can be like for believers when they attempt to live outside of their identity as Crucified Christians. Many scholars point out the fact that Paul does not mention the Holy Spirit in this section as evidence that Paul is displaying the kind of struggle that Christians have when they live without the power of the Holy Spirit. Robert Mounce draws the following conclusion:

> I believe that in this section Paul was revealing with considerable candor his difficulty in meeting the radical demands of the Christian faith. At the same time, he was using his own experience to describe the inevitability of spiritual defeat whenever a believer fails to appropriate the Spirit of God for victory.[10]

Another option that could resolve the tension of these verses is that Paul is not describing the Crucified Lifestyle at all. Instead, he could be attempting to illustrate the struggle that a person has when they try to become righteous by obeying the Law. As a Pharisee, Paul would be very familiar with how impossible it was to fully obey the demands of the Torah, due to his sinful nature rising up in response to his attempts. It is plausible that Paul is describing the battle that he experienced before conversion. After all, he was already speaking about his experience with the Law and how it revealed his sin earlier in Romans 7. It would be a natural progression to describe the tension in which he used to live. It is as if he is saying, "Now that I've given you a theological explanation, let me explain what that struggle was like in my everyday life." This perspective responds to the inconsistency of Paul's tone by asserting that he was not attempting to illustrate the life of a true believer. Verses 24-25 seem to support this view when Paul states: "O wretched man that I am! Who will deliver me from this body of death? I thank God—through Jesus Christ our Lord!" Mounce summarizes this viewpoint:

> A strong argument against the opposing position (that Paul was describing his spiritual experience as a Christian) is the question that must be raised regarding the real value of a conversion that

leads into a spiritual quagmire of such impotence and misery. How could this be the abundant life that Jesus came to bring?[11]

The honest student of the Bible will have to admit that there are strengths and weaknesses on either side of the argument. In fact, some have even tried to resolve this confusion by suggesting that someone other than Paul later added that section to his letter in order to prove a point. But for our purposes, I want to suggest that what is *most* important about this section of Scripture is not whether Paul was talking about his life before or after his conversion experience, but rather, where are we to find our identity as Crucified Christians?

## WALKING ACCORDING TO THE SPIRIT

Before we draw some final conclusions, let us examine Paul's train of thought immediately following this portion of his letter at the end of Romans 7. He opens chapter 8 with this assertion, "There is therefore now no condemnation to those who are in Christ Jesus, who do not walk according to the flesh, but according to the Spirit." (vs. 1) Here Paul introduces a concept that he expounds upon throughout chapter 8: the believer's choice to live either according to the flesh or according to the Spirit. Paul goes on to explain that what the Law had been unable to do (make people righteous), Jesus did by fulfilling the Law and condemning sin in the flesh. (vss. 3-4) He then describes the difference between those who try to live in the power of their own flesh and those who live a life empowered by the Holy Spirit. There is a stark contrast between the two, as displayed in the following verses:

> For those who live according to the flesh set their minds on the things of the flesh, but those who live according to the Spirit, the things of the Spirit. For to be carnally minded is death, but to be spiritually minded is life and peace. Because the carnal mind is enmity against God; for it is not subject to the law of God, nor

indeed can be. So then, those who are in the flesh cannot please God. (vss. 5-8)

In Romans 8, Paul is showing us how the truths of Romans 6 can be actualized in the life of a believer. How can we live a life that is crucified to sin? And how can we overcome when the power of sin is so strong and our flesh is so weak? The answer is the Spirit-empowered life that Paul is describing. In fact, he states emphatically in verse 9, "But you are not in the flesh but in the Spirit, if indeed the Spirit of God dwells in you." Notice, he speaks to Crucified Christians and says that we are not those who walk according to the flesh. His assumption is that the Holy Spirit that indwells the believer will be the dominating force in our lives. If someone is living in the flesh, they are not living the Crucified Lifestyle afforded to us by Jesus' work on the cross.

In verse 11, Paul declares, "But if the Spirit of Him who raised Jesus from the dead dwells in you, He who raised Christ from the dead will also give life to your mortal bodies through His Spirit who dwells in you." As we read these verses, we are back in familiar territory with Paul's tone being one of exhortation and encouragement. He is no longer describing a hopeless battle against sin, but telling believers that we have the same Spirit alive in us who raised Christ from the dead, and because of this we are not to live according to our flesh. (vs. 12)

He summarizes the section this way, "For if you live according to the flesh you will die; but if by the Spirit you put to death the deeds of the body, you will live." (vs. 13) Paul tells us that the power of the Holy Spirit living inside of us enables us to die to sin and fleshly desires. He uses this victorious language to show us that sin is defeated through the cross. This is the power that God has given us to live the Crucified Lifestyle.

## IN WHICH CHAPTER WILL YOU FIND YOURSELF?

Let me provide a caveat to this discussion. I understand the reality that sin is *possible* in the life of a believer. Of course, we *can* sin. And yes, we do sin. This is why forgiveness and repentance are ongoing needs for the

THREE: CRUCIFIED TO SIN

believer. But the question I want to answer is, "Should we live our lives as believers with the expectation of sin's continual control over us?" I cannot provide all the answers to the questions that have been asked of Romans 7 by biblical scholars. But I am not nearly as concerned about taking a theological stance as I am about revealing the glorious position that we have as Crucified Christians!

The reason this is so important is because Romans 7 is the place that many believers turn to in order to comfort themselves in their proclivity to sin. I have been guilty of this myself. I was once in a continual struggle with habitual sin after conversion. I wanted to believe that this passage described the normal Christian life because it lined up with my own experience. I found solace in this passage. I would read these verses and think, "My sinful lifestyle is not such a big deal to God. Look at Paul. He was constantly giving over to sin too!"

However, we should never approach Scripture with the motivation of making it agree with our beliefs or experiences. If our preconceived idea is unbiblical, finding passages that seem to back up our beliefs will only deceive us further and prevent us from receiving the truth. But now that I have walked through repentance and experienced freedom from sin, I do not believe that the Holy Spirit included this passage in the Bible so that we could feel more comfortable in a life dominated by sin's power. It would be completely incongruent with the New Testament and would contradict what Paul himself taught about the Crucified Lifestyle.

When I discovered that these passages were not a license to sin, I began to realize the necessity of finding my identity in Romans 6 and 8. I believe they are Paul's description of the life that we are to expect from the Lord. When we sin, we are not living in our identity in Christ as Crucified Christians. Because of this, sin in the life of a believer should be an exception, not an expectation.

What you expect has huge implications in what you experience. If you live your life with the expectation that you will sin all the time, you will not be surprised if your life is dominated by sinful habits. Your attitude will be, "Well, that's just how life is. One day in heaven, I'll be free. But I can't expect much more on this side of eternity." However, if you live with the expectation that you are dead to sin, then if you do give in to temptation,

69

you will think, "I shouldn't have done that. And I don't have to. That's not my identity in Christ."

If you read through these three chapters in Romans in order to understand the believer's relationship with sin, it is important to read them in the context of Paul's line of thinking. I want to suggest that the latter half of Romans 7 is not the self-portrait of a Christian who is living the Crucified Lifestyle. I believe we are supposed to find our Crucified identity in the surrounding verses and chapters.

When we think about the concept of sin, let us always remember that the cross is powerful enough to set us free completely from sin's power! Let us choose to keep the goal of a sin-free life, with the realization that, while we will never achieve that fully, God has given us His Spirit and His grace to empower us to live an overcoming life. Let us never lower the standard of holiness to less than the Scriptures demand.

## STAY ON THE CROSS

I once heard a story that illustrates this principle. There was a group of Christians who were performing an Easter drama. One man—who was portraying Jesus—was going to be tied to a cross by soldiers. When the curtains were opened, one of the soldiers was supposed to pretend to spit into the man's face. The night of the drama came. The actors playing the role of the soldiers tied this man's arms and legs to the cross using ropes. The moment arrived to begin the scene and the curtains were drawn. Right on cue, the soldier turned and spit in Jesus' face. However, instead of pretending, the actor actually spit. The man on the cross hissed at the soldier under his breath, "You just wait until I come off of this cross. I'll get you for this!"[12]

Just like this man, we are often tempted to come down off the cross in order to sin. Paul says, "Reckon yourselves to be dead indeed to sin."[13] But as Christians, we are not always willing to do that. We get in the flesh. We want to handle things our own way rather than submitting to the Lord. Living the Crucified Lifestyle requires us to choose to stay on the cross. When we step down off the cross to sin, we are essentially leaving Romans

6 and 8 truths and choosing to live in the latter half of Romans 7. The question we need to answer every day is, "In which portion of Romans 6-8 will I find my identity? The sin-controlled lifestyle or the Crucified Lifestyle?" The choice is ours to make.

In the next chapter, we will discuss another powerful force that the cross has made us victorious over—the world system.

"The best means of resisting the devil is, to destroy whatever of the world remains in us, in order to raise for God, upon its ruins, a building all of love."

-John Wesley[1]

# CHAPTER

# 4

## CRUCIFIED TO THE WORLD

*Crucified Christians are Set Apart from the World System*

WE LIVE IN REMARKABLE TIMES as twenty-first century believers, especially as it relates to the world around us. With the breathtaking advancement of technology, the world system is more easily accessible than it has ever been. Never has the world had more entry points into our lives than it does today. Because of the internet, media, smartphones and other gadgets, most of us have access to immediate updates on the latest world events, as well as an endless assortment of audio, video and written content about any subject one can imagine. When we look back to what the world was like sixty or seventy years ago, it really is astounding to see how much humans have achieved in the arena of technology. It makes you wonder what the world could look like fifty years from now.

In Galatians 6:14, Paul makes a significant statement:

But God forbid that I should boast except in the cross of our Lord Jesus Christ, by whom the world has been crucified to me, and I to the world.

This verse reveals to us another relationship that is severed by the cross when we are born again. Not only are Crucified Christians dead to the power of sin, but also to the world system and all it has to offer.

## A RELENTLESS ATTACK

The influence of the world is increasing at an alarming rate. Unfortunately, it is not only the unbelieving world that is riveted by the technology and information craze of our time. The church—especially in the West—has gotten caught up in the pursuit as well. In doing so, we have allowed the world to have greater influence over our lives. The spirit of the world is calling out for our attention more adamantly than we have seen in history; it is trying to find any possible avenue into our hearts.

Recently, I noticed a hole had been dug in the garden bed by our front porch. An animal had attempted to burrow into the open space underneath, and based on the size of the hole, it was probably successful. I tried to fill the hole with dirt, hoping that the animal had exited, and I had not trapped it under the porch. A couple of days later, I noticed a similar hole in another place. I put a rock in front of that hole and soon discovered another one just a few feet away. It seemed that no matter what I did, the animal managed to make another pathway. It was relentless in its attempts to access the space under our porch.

The world system is a lot like that animal, trying to find access into a Christian's heart any way that it can. If we close one door to the world, it will try to enter through another. The spirit of this world does not care how it gains access to our hearts; it simply wants in. We cannot expect any half-hearted attempts at resistance to be successful. A lackadaisical approach to our relationship with the world is insufficient. If ever there was a time period in history when the church should be diligently separating itself from the world system, it is in our day.

## THE PROCESS OF SEPARATION

Separation describes the action of putting distance between two objects. Picture a glass of water and a teaspoon of salt sitting on a table. These are two distinct substances. If I were to take the salt, pour it into the glass and stir it, the salt crystals would dissolve and become one substance: saltwater. While the salt and water are combined, I cannot reach into the glass and pull out a salt crystal because the two distinct elements have become one. The only way to separate the two substances again is through a chemical process, such as evaporation. When water evaporates, it turns into vapor, leaving behind the salt in the jar and the two substances are once again distinct from each other.

This is an illustration of what happens in the hearts of Christians who allow the world into their lives. When believers join themselves with the world system in some way, it becomes a part of who they are. Their lifestyle is adapted to accommodate the world, affecting how they think, feel and act. They essentially grow comfortable living in the "gray area" between holiness and worldliness. The lines become blurred, and their spiritual lives are like the saltwater in our example, joined to the world system. However, through intentional distancing from the world, they can once again experience freedom from its influence and control. Spiritual separation gives us the ability to draw a dividing line between ourselves and the world as an act of consecration unto the Lord.

## LEGALISM VS. HOLINESS

It is important that we make a distinction between legalistic separation and the separation that comes with holiness. *Legalism* can be defined as, "close attention to the stated requirements of the law, without regard to their intention (i.e. attention to the letter of the law rather than to the spirit of the law)."[2] If a believer chooses to separate from the world with a self-righteous attitude, or due to a sense of guilt or condemnation, it becomes legalism. But not all separation is legalistic. Instead, it can be an integral part of developing a holy lifestyle. The pursuit of true holiness must always take place in cooperation with God. The Holy Spirit is faithful to convict us when He sees compromise in our lives. When we respond with separation motivated by obedience to His conviction, the result is a lifestyle of increasing holiness.

Spiritual separation has two elements. First, we separate *from* something. We choose to discontinue a worldly activity when we realize it brings compromise or imbalance into our lives. But this is only the first part of the equation. We also need to turn *toward* the Lord, by intentionally pursuing Him with renewed vigor. The purpose of separating from the world should always be to draw near to God. So, it is not only that we rid our lives of worldly attachments, but we must fill them with disciplines that strengthen our relationship with the Lord. This will help safeguard us from legalism.

Separation is not about writing a list of do's and don'ts and telling everyone to follow it. It is not something that we can work up in our own strength. Rather, it is something that we do in the context of relationship with the Lord under His guidance and the Holy Spirit's leading. We do not trust in the separation itself to make us holy. Instead, because we desire to live a holy life for God, we choose to allow Him to lead us in consecrating our lives to Him. Holiness is a lifestyle that comes as a result of true relationship. Our heart's cry should be, "I do not want to have *anything* in my life that negatively impacts my relationship with my Heavenly Father."

## OUR ASSOCIATION WITH THE WORLD

When it comes to the concept of separation, some church cultures practice it by distancing themselves from worldly people. The belief is that Christians should isolate themselves from all relationships with unbelievers in order to insulate themselves from their ungodly influence. However, when we have little or no contact with the world around us, we end up in a Christian bubble and we lose our ability to be a witness to others. We are called to be the light of the world,[3] which requires us to shine in the darkness. Paul did talk about separating from people at times, but listen to what he says to the Corinthian church in his first letter to them:

> I wrote to you in my letter not to associate with sexually immoral people—not at all meaning the people of this world who are immoral, or the greedy and swindlers, or idolaters. In that case you would have to leave this world. But now I am writing to you that you must not associate with anyone who claims to be a brother or sister but is sexually immoral or greedy, an idolater or slanderer, a drunkard or swindler. Do not even eat with such people.
> **(1 Corinthians 5:9-11 NIV)**

Here, Paul is saying, "When I talk about separating from certain sinful people, I'm not suggesting you stay away from the sinners of this world, because they will always be around. I'm talking about distancing yourselves from people who claim to be Christians yet live in unrepentant sin."

In another passage, Paul does warn the church, "Do not be yoked together with unbelievers. For what do righteousness and wickedness have in common? Or what fellowship can light have with darkness?"[4] This is talking about having the type of intimate relationship with an unbeliever in which you are mutually influencing one another. It is wise for us to avoid heart connections with people which can lead us away from the Lord. But that does not mean we are not to associate with the world at all. Instead, when the New Testament uses the term *world*, it is not primarily referring to people, but rather the world system.

## DEFINING KOSMOS

The Bible makes many strong statements about a Christian's relationship with the world. Two pointed warnings about loving the world come from James and John:

> Adulterers and adulteresses! Do you not know that friendship with the world is enmity with God? Whoever therefore wants to be a friend of the world makes himself an enemy of God. (**James 4:4**)

> Do not love the world or the things in the world. If anyone loves the world, the love of the Father is not in him. (**1 John 2:15**)

We all have a mental filter that affects how we interpret these verses. I used to assume these passages meant that we were not to curse, go to bars and sleep around. After all, this was my stereotype of what a "worldly" person would be like. If you ask five different Christians how they define the term *world* in this passage, I suppose you might get five different answers, all containing a measure of truth. But when we research the Greek word *kosmos*, we find a much broader concept of the world than might be commonly understood. One commentary defines kosmos this way:

> Ethically, morally, or spiritually, the present world-order or system of life in its condition of self-reliance and independence from God…Kosmos as such is concerned with the present, transitory dimension of life, ignoring or denying eternity, gauging existence by material standards and defining achievement in terms of human esteem…which reflect the man-centered spirit of this world.[5]

We see from this definition that the term *kosmos* encompasses more than doing drugs, sleeping around and living a life of moral compromise. Of course, it would include those types of behavior. But the term for *world* used in these passages is much more comprehensive than that. Kosmos is essentially referring to the world system that exists outside of the rule of God and relationship with Him. Steve Gallagher writes the following about kosmos:

> Although sometimes the word refers to everyone living on the planet earth, it is used primarily to describe the *corporate consciousness* of the people of this world who are in rebellion against God's authority. *Kosmos* is what binds together the unbelieving world. It is a global mentality that remains a powerful

unspoken force in the lives of mankind. It molds vastly different people groups into one entity which lives out its existence on earth under the domain of Satan, *unified against God.*⁶*

If we tend to read the warnings from James and John with a flippant attitude, assuming they do not apply to us, perhaps we should take a closer look at what kosmos entails.

## THE PHILOSOPHIES OF KOSMOS

Kosmos includes a set of philosophies that form a distinctive worldview. A worldview is defined as, "a comprehensive conception or apprehension of the world especially from a specific standpoint."⁷ Every worldview has a predetermined set of beliefs. For example, the Christian worldview would include such beliefs as the existence of God, eternity and the truths of the Bible. The secular worldview of kosmos has its own philosophies that are shared by most who operate within its system. Three of these philosophies are humanism, atheism and hedonism and are manifestations of kosmos found especially in Western culture.

*Humanism* is "a philosophy that usually rejects supernaturalism and stresses an individual's dignity and worth and capacity for self-realization through reason."⁸ Science and human intellect become the primary means for understanding the world around us from this philosophy of life. Basically, humanism puts humans on a pedestal as the center of the universe. The focus is not on the Creator, but on the creation. Romans 1:25 speaks about people who, "exchanged the truth of God for the lie, and worshiped and served the creature rather than the Creator." This is an excellent biblical description of humanism.

*Atheism* is closely linked to humanism. In the broadest sense, atheism is, "a lack of belief or a strong disbelief in the existence of a god or any gods."⁹ This philosophy approaches life with the basic foundational premise that there is no God and, therefore, no spiritual world. Atheism teaches that the

---

*I owe a tremendous debt to Steve Gallagher regarding my understanding of kosmos. His book *Intoxicated with Babylon* is a must read on this topic.

physical dimension of life is all that exists and there is no afterlife. The theory of evolution is an atheistic attempt to explain how the world could come into existence apart from the Creator. Practices that devalue life, such as abortion or euthanasia, are the results of a worldview that does not believe in God, and therefore, claims that we have no accountability to Him.

A third philosophy integral to the kosmos worldview is hedonism, which is, "the doctrine that pleasure or happiness is the sole or chief good in life."[10] *Hedonism* teaches that—as humans—we have a right to pursue personal happiness, even at the expense of others. It is the philosophy behind the modern-day belief that morality is subjective. With a hedonistic approach to life, you have no basis for telling me that something I am doing is wrong if it makes me happy. The thought behind this philosophy is, "Live your life to the fullest. Do what feels good." Or, as Solomon once wrote, "A man has nothing better under the sun than to eat, drink and be merry."[11]

These are three of the philosophies that describe the secular world's way of thinking. And you can observe all of them being manifested in areas of modern society, such as Hollywood, the music industry, government and advertising. People who are influenced by the philosophies of kosmos speak, create and live according to these man-centered expressions of life. Western society is so deeply entrenched in these philosophies that many people accept them as truth without even questioning their credibility.

## WORLDLINESS AT OUR DOOR

The issue with worldliness in the modern-day church is that many have allowed kosmos to infiltrate their lives and they cannot see it. The church is being lulled to sleep by the spirit of this world. As Andrew Bonar once declared, "I looked for the church, I found it in the world. I looked for the world, I found it in the church."[12] What is shocking about this statement is that he said this back in the 1800s!

Andrew Bonar was not the only person in Christian history to be deeply troubled by the worldliness of the church of his day. Hannah Whitall Smith—who lived from 1832-1911—made this statement:

For the most part, the followers of Jesus Christ are satisfied with a life so conformed to the world, and so like it in almost every respect, that to a casual observer, no difference is discernable.[13]

It amazes me that these quotes came from a time in history even before the invention of television. These believers were concerned about worldliness in the church at a time when technology was rudimentary and the world system was seemingly much more innocent. What would Andrew Bonar and Hannah Whitall Smith say if they were living today? How would they feel about the way most Christians live in Western society?

Watchman Nee expressed his own concern in the book, *Love Not the World*:

The time has passed when we need to go out into the world in order to make contact with it. Today the world comes and searches us out. There is a force abroad now which is captivating men. Have you ever felt the power of the world as much as today?…Wherever you go, even among Christians, the things of the world are the topics of conversation. The world has advanced to the very door of the Church and is seeking to draw even the saints of God into its grasp. Never in this sphere of things have we needed to know the power of the Cross of Christ to deliver us as we do at the present time.[14]

I would venture to say that the draw of kosmos has not weakened since he spoke those words over fifty years ago. These saints would have us ask the question today, "Have we allowed a coalescence of the church and the world system to form because of our refusal to take kosmos seriously?"

## INFLUENCED BY KOSMOS

The reason that the world's influence is so dangerous is because it shapes how we think and how we view life. The Bible teaches us, "Do not be conformed to this world, but be transformed by the renewing of your mind."¹⁵ The Greek for *conformed* is *suschēmatizō* and means to assume "a similar outward form by following the same pattern."¹⁶ Paul warns us to make sure we are not patterning our lives in the same mold as the world. Instead, we are to go through a transformation process, resulting in our minds being renewed. This takes place as we spend time receiving truth from the Lord and being influenced by His worldview. It occurs when we read, memorize, study and meditate upon the Word of God. But how many Christians in the church spend less than a few minutes a day in the Bible and several hours receiving from the world system? Whether we realize it or not, when we turn on the television, surf the internet, check out the news, read a book or listen to secular music, we are meditating on its message.

I had an experience recently that left me pondering this concept of meditation. In order to understand this story, I have to explain that I have a mind like a steel trap. There is something about the way my brain works that stores information—especially music—whether I want it to or not. Because of this, I have the entire musical scores of several Disney movies stored in my brain and I can recite the lyrics at will (not a talent that ever comes in handy). I can remember jingles from commercials and nursery rhymes from my childhood word-for-word.

A couple of years ago, we were with some of my family down in Florida and we took our kids to a water park. I was sitting in a lawn chair with my youngest daughter sleeping in my arms. I was forced to sit there with worldly music blaring in my ears. I tried my best to tune it out, but it proved to be a futile effort. A pop song came on and something about the beat and the singing style gripped me. As annoying as it was, I memorized the chorus without even trying. It was stuck in my head for a couple of weeks and took intentional effort to get it to go away.

Months later, I was sitting in line at a bank to make a deposit and that song came on the radio. "Oh no," I thought to myself, "this song is going to be in my head for another two weeks!" Although frustrated, I stood there in line and began to listen to the lyrics. I could hear the hurt and pain in the words of the young girl who wrote the song. It occurred to me in those few moments that, by listening to the song, I was entering into her world.

I had a revelation standing in that bank about how the world system works. It comes to us with a message, which is established and communicated by someone with an agenda. And when we watch, read, view or listen to secular media, we are entering into the worldview of the one who created it. That message will influence our thinking, affect our emotions and impact our lives in many ways. Yet, as Christians, we should seek to be influenced by God's agenda and worldview.

## THE CORRUPTION OF MEDIA

The world system uses a variety of methods to influence us. While media and entertainment are not the only ones, I want to address them specifically because they seem to be a common issue in the Western church world. What people watch on screens today would have been appalling in the early days of the entertainment industry. In fact, the Motion Picture Production Code, introduced in 1930, included the following guiding principle for filmmaking:

> No picture shall be produced which will lower the moral standards of those who see it. Hence the sympathy of the audience should never be thrown to the side of crime, wrongdoing, evil or sin.[17]

Think of how far we have fallen from those days! The more we are exposed to sin and darkness as a society, the greater our level of desensitization. Once the industry pushes a little deeper into immorality, it cannot turn back. It has created an audience that demands greater thrills, more graphic violence, deeper perversion and visual stimulation with each new release.

There is a lack of clean, moral programming in the entertainment arena. Although Christian companies are beginning to produce quality entertainment, they are still an extreme minority and do not receive anywhere near the attention that other media does. Entertainment companies exist to acquire people's money, so what the people demand is what they produce. If the majority of people in the West demanded clean, family-friendly shows, this is what would dominate television and movie theaters. But that is obviously not the case. As the moral compass of our society slips into greater degradation, so does the moral quality of entertainment.

The danger does not lie merely in the overt immoral behaviors depicted on screens. There is a much more subtle threat that many never stop to consider: the illusion that people can have fulfilling, happy and peaceful lives without Christ. Even the innocent programming that existed in the early years of television mostly portrayed a life where Jesus was not the center. The sweetest love stories of Hollywood or Disney cartoons attempt to convey stories where everything works out with a happy ending. Yet, without Christ, there are no happy endings! We are being lied to by the humanistic, atheistic and hedonistic philosophies of kosmos on a regular basis. But many in the church have grown so accustomed to it, they do not ever step far enough away to really examine what they are allowing into their lives.

I am not saying that all secular entertainment is going to corrupt our faith or needs to be completely eradicated from our lives. I thank God that there are companies that still produce content with family-friendly values. But when we are constantly feeding ourselves and our families with entertainment devoid of Christ, we are unconsciously training our minds to think the way the world does. I think it is important that we take a step back and consider the underlying message of anything we allow into our lives. Kosmos wants us to keep our minds on this world, while the Scriptures tell us to keep our minds on eternal things.[18] We have a responsibility to be aware of the content that we are consuming and the way it impacts us, and to separate ourselves from anything that is pulling us away from intimacy with God.

## WASTING TIME IN THE WORLD

Beyond the immorality and godlessness that is too common in worldly content, we also ought to consider the sheer amount of wasted time attached to our engagement with it. One survey revealed that the average modern American adult spends "over 11 hours per day listening to, watching, reading or generally interacting with media."[19] That adds up to 4,015 hours a year. When calculating the average time Americans spend on their smartphones, statistics show a daily average of close to four hours for adults.[20] When you consider these staggering statistics, they should be a sober reminder for believers to examine how well we are stewarding our valuable time here on the earth. The wasted time alone should cause us to think twice about how much of the world we are consuming.

One day, we will all stand before Christ to give an account of our lives.[21] If it is true that we will have to give an explanation for every careless word spoken,[22] will we not also have to give an account for wasted time? How many Christians will stand before the Lord on that day, having to admit that they squandered much of their lives on things that did not really matter? But that does not have to be our testimony. We can make a choice to alter our lifestyles to allow for a greater pursuit of eternal things.

## DEVELOPING PERSONAL BOUNDARIES

Early in our marriage, my wife and I used to be much less cautious about the entertainment we enjoyed. To some degree, we did make an effort to limit ourselves to content that was not too violent, sexual or profane. In fact, we thought we were exercising wisdom because we seemed to be more cautious than many of our Christian friends. But in hindsight, the way we made our decisions was based more on our own feelings and less about what the Word of God teaches.

Filtering content based on conscience might seem like a wise way to live, except that our feelings are not always dependable. Have you ever spoken to a professing Christian who has sin in their lives, and their defense is, "I don't feel convicted about it"? You would tell them, "It doesn't matter how you feel about something if the Bible clearly calls it sin." Our conscience can lie to us, which is why we need to live according to biblical principles. Our hearts and minds can become desensitized, which makes them an unreliable filter.

I think the average Christian has at least some boundaries they are unwilling to cross when it comes to entertainment. The problem comes when we leave it up to ourselves to decide where that line should be drawn.

People will say, "Well, there is only a little cursing, nudity or violence in this movie, so I don't think it's too bad to watch." When our filter is based on human wisdom, it can easily lead a Christian down the slippery slope of trying to get as close to sin as possible, without crossing the line of overt compromise. It creates gray moral areas that blur the lines between sin and holiness. Our flesh longs for entertainment that is thrilling, comedic, sensuous and captivating. If we are depending on the flesh to help us walk in holiness, it will never happen.

Imagine I handed you a bottle of water because you are thirsty. Right before you take a sip, I tell you, "Just so you know, I did put a drop of ether in there." You look at the water, and it appears to be perfectly normal. Would you drink that water knowing that there is poison in it, even if you were incredibly thirsty? Of course not. Because you know there is no way to only drink the water, since the two substances are combined. Yet, this is the kind of logic that Christians often use when it comes to what the world offers us: "A little sin is no big deal. I can pick and choose what I allow to affect me."

We each need to learn what it means to walk in the Spirit regarding our relationship with the world system. Paul tells us in 2 Corinthians 7:1, "Let us cleanse ourselves from all filthiness of the flesh and spirit, perfecting holiness in the fear of God." The writer of Hebrews exhorts us to make every effort to be holy.[23] We should do everything in our power to live a holy life. If there is anything that is contaminating our lives with the spirit of this world, the proper response is separation.

For our family, cutting out television and most secular media has been one of the greatest spiritual decisions that we have made. It has profoundly impacted the way we live and has helped us grow spiritually. We still have to make decisions on a regular basis about what to allow our children to watch, listen to and read. But seeing the reality of kosmos has helped us to eliminate significant compromise from our lives. Perhaps this is a more drastic step than the Lord would ask you to take. But the question that needs to be answered is are you willing to if He does?

You might think to yourself, "Why would God ask me to do something radical about the world's influence in my life? No one else in the church is living like that." The words of an old Gospel tract called, "Others May, You Cannot" might help to answer that question:

> If God has called you to be really like Jesus, He will draw you into a life of crucifixion and humility, and put upon you such demands of obedience, that you will not be able to follow other people, or measure yourself by other Christians, and in many ways He will seem to let other good people do things which He will not let you do.
>
> The Holy Spirit will put a strict watch over you, with a jealous love, and will rebuke you for little words and feelings, or for wasting your time, which other Christians never seem distressed over. So make up your mind that God is an infinite Sovereign, and has a right to do as He pleases with His own. He may not explain to you a thousand things which puzzle your reason in His dealings with you, but if you absolutely sell yourself to be His love slave, He will wrap you up in a jealous love, and bestow upon you many blessings which come only to those who are in the inner circle.
>
> Settle it forever, then, that you are to deal directly with the Holy Spirit, and that He is to have the privilege of tying your tongue, or chaining your hand, or closing your eyes, in ways that He does not seem to use with others. Now when you are so possessed with the loving God that you are, in your secret heart, pleased and delighted over this peculiar, personal, private, jealous guardianship and management of the Holy Spirit over your life, you will have found the vestibule of Heaven.[24]

As we endeavor to live the Crucified Lifestyle, we will find that the Lord will keep a tighter rein on our thoughts, actions, attitudes and lifestyles. This is not something to be resisted but treasured.

## EVALUATING ENTERTAINMENT BIBLICALLY

Perhaps the Lord is tugging on your heart in this area, but you do not know where to begin. I want to provide a couple of methods that have assisted us in evaluating entertainment in our lives and deciding what should stay and what should go.

The first is the Philippians test, and comes from Paul's epistle to the church in Philippi, where he writes:

> Finally, brothers and sisters, whatever is true, whatever is noble, whatever is right, whatever is pure, whatever is lovely, whatever is admirable—if anything is excellent or praiseworthy—think about such things.[25]

This passage provides us with an effective filter to judge what we watch, view online, listen to or read. If something we want to be entertained by does not fall into these categories, we should consider making another choice with our time.

The second method of evaluation would be to ask the question, "Does this glorify something for which Jesus had to die?" If the movie, website, video game, book, song, podcast, magazine or television show is bringing glory to things for which Jesus had to pay the ultimate price, how can we find enjoyment in that entertainment? Does it glorify sexual sin? Are the jokes inappropriate? Does it make light of things that God is against? Is it filled with profanity or sexual innuendo? These are the types of questions that sincere seekers of the Crucified Lifestyle ask themselves. When you begin to filter media through these biblical principles, you will discover that much of what the world offers has no place in the life of a believer. It might be pleasing to our flesh, but are we living to please ourselves or to please our God?

## WHAT IS OUR RESPONSE TO BE?

Many Christians will scoff at a teaching like this and call it legalism.

They will say it is just old-fashioned thinking and would reject or ignore it completely. But if the Bible makes such strong statements about not loving the world, should we not at least take a moment to examine our lives and ask the Holy Spirit if there is anything that we should change?

I am not suggesting that a Christian who allows secular entertainment in their lives is going to hell. Nor am I saying that every Christian should go home and smash their televisions, computers, smartphones and other technology. I am also not proposing that getting rid of these things automatically makes us more holy. I am simply saying we should take time to evaluate our lives to make sure we are not compromising our God-given time or values with the world system.

The Crucified Lifestyle requires a careful review of our relationship with the world system. Part of being united with Christ on the cross is that we are crucified to kosmos. We no longer allow the world system and its man-centered thinking to influence our lives. We now live according to the Kingdom of God and its God-centered thinking.

Allow me to close this chapter with a final thought from Andrew Murray:

> It is only through death to the world that we can be freed from its spirit. The separation must be vital and entire. It is only through the acceptance of our crucifixion with Christ that we can live out this confession, and, as crucified to the world, maintain the position of irreconcilable hostility to whatever is of its spirit and not of the spirit of God…The cross, with its shame and its separation from the world, and its death to all that is of flesh and of self, is the only power that can conquer the spirit of the world.[26]

In the next chapter, we will learn about the fear of man, which is a powerful force that seeks to prevent us from embracing the cross-centered life.

"We fear men so much, because we fear God so little."

-William Gurnall[1]

# CHAPTER

# 5

## CRUCIFIED TO THE OPINIONS OF PEOPLE

*Crucified Christians are Motivated by God's Opinion*

**THE CRUCIFIED LIFESTYLE IS NOT** for the cowardly. Nor is it accessible to those who desire to blend into the crowd. It is reserved for those who are willing to swim against the current of popular culture in an effort to please the God they serve. For many of us, the fear of other people's opinions poses a significant challenge as we endeavor to follow Jesus as His disciples. In this chapter, we will discuss our need to be crucified to the fear of man.

*Fear* is defined as, "an unpleasant, often strong emotion caused by anticipation or awareness of danger."[2] Fear is experienced emotionally and is common to the human experience. Fear is not a sin in and of itself but is meant to be a safety impulse to protect us. However, the way that we respond to fear can cause us to sin. The concept of fear is found frequently throughout the Bible. However, when you search through the Scriptures, you will have a difficult time finding any passage that tells us we ought to fear anything or anyone other than the Lord. In contrast, many Scriptures encourage us to resist and overcome fear. God understands that we will deal with the fear of man at times. However, His expectation is that we will choose to trust Him instead of allowing fear to control us.

In order to truly follow Jesus, we will have to accept that not everyone will understand, appreciate and support the way that we live. Jesus Himself told His followers that they would be hated by people because of their relationship with Him.[3] For this reason, Crucified Christians cannot be people-pleasers. Paul once wrote to the church in Galatia, "If I were still trying to please people, I would not be a servant of Christ."[4] That is a strong assertion. The apostle tells us that we cannot truly serve Jesus when we are motivated by the opinions of other people. Which brings us to a question we should all consider: Are we truly living our lives for God's approval alone?

## STUCK IN A SNARE

The fear of man occurs any time we allow the opinions of people to dictate our decisions rather than the opinion of God. If we make decisions based on the question, "What are other people going to think about this?" rather than, "What does God think about this?" we are operating out of the fear of man. Proverbs 29:25 tells us, "The fear of man brings a snare, but whoever trusts in the Lord shall be safe." The Hebrew word used for *snare* is *moqesh*. Its literal meaning is a noose for catching animals.[5] Picture a bear walking carelessly through the forest, when suddenly its foot gets caught in a trap and it is completely immobilized and unable to escape. No matter how much it strains and struggles to break free, it will not be able to move forward unless it can find a way to extract its leg from the trap.

This is a perfect illustration to describe what happens spiritually to Christians when we allow the fear of man to control our lives. It has a crippling effect on us. We might desire to move forward in our walk with the Lord, but it will be impossible if the fear of man is kept wrapped around our spiritual "leg." Just like the bear caught in a trap, Christians who fear the opinions of others will be prevented from moving forward until they can be freed from the snare.

## CURSED OR BLESSED?

A passage in Jeremiah speaks about the fear of man from a different perspective. First, it describes someone who is controlled by others:

> Cursed is the man who trusts in man and makes flesh his strength, whose heart departs from the Lord. For he shall be like a shrub in the desert, and shall not see when good comes, but shall inhabit the parched places in the wilderness, in a salt land which is not inhabited. (Jeremiah 17:5-6)

In this passage, Jeremiah declares that people who put their trust in man are cursed. He describes someone whose primary allegiance is toward other people. This kind of person is compared to a bush that is dry and fruitless. Notice that it says that this person's heart "departs from the Lord." The allegiance of our hearts can only focus in one direction, either toward other people or toward the Lord. We cannot live for the approval of both at the same time. But notice what he goes on to say about the person who trusts in the Lord:

> Blessed is the man who trusts in the Lord, and whose hope is the Lord. For he shall be like a tree planted by the waters, which spreads out its roots by the river, and will not fear when heat comes; but its leaf will be green, and will not be anxious in the year of drought, nor will cease from yielding fruit. (Jeremiah 17:7-8)

The contrast of this second description is stark when juxtaposed with the first person. Here, the person whose heart is loyal to God is seen like a well-watered tree, bursting with fruit, and able to withstand trials. Jeremiah says that this type of man has no fear when the heat comes. Even when he is walking through the fire, he does not burn up. Rather, he never fails to bear fruit.

When you consider these two illustrations, which would you want to define your life? Do you desire to live a cursed or a blessed life? You and I have the ability to choose between the two. And the dividing factor between them is whether we fear man or God.

## JEREMIAH'S CALL

Understanding more about the life of Jeremiah makes these verses much more profound. When the Lord called Jeremiah into his prophetic ministry, He warned him in advance about the challenges he would face from other people. God encouraged Jeremiah to say whatever he was commanded, without fear of what men would try to do to him. The Lord instructed the prophet, "They will fight against you but will not overcome you, for I am with you and will rescue you."[6]

This is not the kind of warning that anyone would want to receive from the Lord. God is telling Jeremiah, "Your ministry is going to be really difficult. People aren't going to like what you have to say. But I'll be with you. So, although you will be tempted to fear, don't give in to it." I wonder what was going through Jeremiah's mind at the time that he received that word. He might have been wondering if there was someone else more qualified whom the Lord could use instead.

In one particularly tumultuous season of ministry, Jeremiah was under intense persecution. His enemies were even plotting to put him to death.[7] During that time, Jeremiah complained to the Lord about the trial he was walking through. Which of us could blame him for the way he felt? If we were going through similar circumstances, we would feel justified in complaining to the Lord as well. But when the Lord answered Jeremiah, He said something unexpected:

> If you have run with the footmen, and they have wearied you, then how can you contend with horses? And if in the land of peace, in

which you trusted, they wearied you, then how will you do in the floodplain of the Jordan? **(Jeremiah 12:5)**

God basically rebukes His prophet for allowing men to wear him down. Even though it was obviously a challenging situation, the Lord does not pat Jeremiah on the back and tell him everything is going to be alright. Instead, He asks a pointed question, "If you are caving in with these situations, how will you survive when things get really tough?"

I think the Lord would say the same thing to many in the Western church today. If we have no spiritual backbone now, what makes us think that we can survive intense persecution against our faith? If we are crippled by fear when people in our workplace judge us for being Christians, how will we stay faithful when it might cost us our lives to identify with Jesus? The Christian life cannot be lived properly when we are operating out of fear. We need to be willing to press through our fear and live in the fear of the Lord.

## THE INEVITABILITY OF OPPOSITION

While Jeremiah's story might be an extreme example, I think most Christians can relate to facing some degree of opposition for their faith. Serving God will bring us into dispute with other people; it is simply par for the course. 2 Timothy 3:12 tells us, "All who desire to live godly in Christ Jesus will suffer persecution." This is one of the Bible promises that most of us prefer not to dwell on. Nevertheless, experiencing pushback from others is part of every disciple's journey.

It is easy to proclaim Christ when we are in church and surrounded by our Christian friends and family. There is no risk when we talk about Him with people who share our worldview. However, when we are in a situation where we might be ridiculed or rejected, suddenly we are tempted to cower. Fear can cause us to never speak the truth due to fear of backlash.

If you have not experienced any opposition for your faith in Christ, you probably do not spend much time in evangelism. When we share the Gospel, it does not take long for someone to get upset, no matter how tactful or loving our approach. The message of the cross is offensive to human nature. Certainly, there are times when we might be too abrasive, or deliver the message in the wrong spirit. However, even if the right message is expressed in the proper way, the Gospel message we carry will cause offense in people who choose to resist it. Because of the fear of potential opposition, many believers miss out on the exciting adventure of sharing the Gospel and winning souls for the Lord. The fear of man can prevent us from experiencing the rich life that Jesus has in store for us.

## PETER'S FEAR OF MAN

The Apostle Peter's story provides us with hope that we do not have to allow the opinions of people to cripple us permanently. Peter was a man who wrestled with the fear of other people on more than one occasion. Yet, he leaves us a legacy of a man who lived boldly for Jesus. History even records that he was crucified upside down on a cross because he did not feel worthy to die like his master.[8] Though Peter had struggled with fear throughout his journey, he finished strong for the glory of God!

One example of Peter's battle with the fear of man occurred on the night that Jesus was crucified. At the last supper, Peter had boldly declared to Jesus: "Even if I have to die with You, I will not deny You!"[9] I am certain that Peter had good intentions. He wanted to publicly affirm his unconditional loyalty to his leader. However, Jesus already knew that Peter would not stay true to his word. And it was not long until Peter's confident assertion was tested.

Once Jesus had been arrested, and His disciples had scattered, we find Peter warming his hands by a fire, trying to follow Jesus at a distance to see what would transpire. Matthew records that a servant girl questioned Peter about his connection with Christ and he publicly denied it. He then repeated the same response to another servant girl and even swore to a group of people that he did not know Jesus at all.[10]

Peter had a brash personality. He was known for speaking his mind freely, often resulting in careless and overly zealous words. Yet, on the night Jesus headed toward the cross, Peter denied his identity as a disciple.

This grown man who usually seemed strong and courageous cowered in the fear of man. And the reason for Peter's denial was because he did not want to be associated with Jesus when it might cost him something he was unwilling to pay. Peter realized his life could be threatened if he admitted to following Jesus, so he caved, not only once, but three times. And before you and I judge him for this moment of weakness, let us consider how often we too stay silent when being known as a Christ follower might cost us something we are not willing to pay ourselves.

## PETER AND PAUL

This is not the only story we have of Peter succumbing to the fear of man. In his letter to the Galatian Christians, the Apostle Paul recounted the story of a time when he needed to rebuke Peter for hypocrisy. Peter had made a habit of eating together with Gentiles who had become Christians. Culturally, most Jewish people at that time would find the practice of intermingling with Gentiles unacceptable due to their understanding of the Law. But the Holy Spirit had revealed to both Peter and Paul that God desired the Gospel to be made available to all people, including the Gentiles.[11]

One day, some men who belonged to a group that believed that Gentiles needed to be circumcised according to the Law in order to be converted came to visit. When they arrived, Peter began to separate himself from the Gentiles during meals because of his fear of their opinion. This became such a problem that other Jews including Barnabas also joined him in distancing themselves from the Gentile Christians. Paul ended up calling Peter out in front of everyone. He wrote:

> But when I saw that they were not straightforward about the truth of the gospel, I said to Peter before them all, "If you, being a Jew, live in the manner of Gentiles and not as the Jews, why do you compel Gentiles to live as Jews?" **(Galatians 2:14)**

Peter had normally chosen to eat with the Gentile believers based on his personal convictions. However, when there were people around him who believed differently, Peter allowed the fear of man to change the way he lived. Unlike the night that Jesus was betrayed, Peter was not afraid for his life in this situation. Rather, this is an example of Peter trying to avoid confrontation from within the church. He struggled with being overly concerned about what others thought about him.

If we are honest, most of us can identify with Peter's battle. Despite his ongoing struggle with the fear of man, on the Day of Pentecost, the Holy Spirit came upon Peter, and he had the opportunity to preach a powerful message that brought three thousand people to the faith.[12] Peter serves as a clear example that even those who have battled with the fear of man can still be used mightily in the Kingdom of God. Let us learn from Peter's example and refuse to allow our past failures in this area to cripple our future.

## PERSECUTED FOR HOLINESS' SAKE

Part of living the Crucified Lifestyle is accepting the fact that embracing it can sometimes bring us into conflict with other Christians. When we choose to live a sold-out life for Jesus, others in the church who have lost their first love[13] can become our biggest persecutors. The presence of spiritual hunger in one person reveals lukewarmness in another.

The priorities of the Crucified Lifestyle demand that those who pursue it live differently than the average professing Christian in the Western church. In light of the previous chapter about separation from the world system, consider the experience of a young man named John. He is a college student and part of a local church body. John has a group of friends who frequent movie theaters together as a hobby. As movie buffs, they stay current with the latest news on the film industry and are always anticipating upcoming releases.

One weekend, John goes to a Christian conference. During this time with the Lord, he begins to experience conviction about the types of movies he watches with his friends. For the first time, he really reflects on the questionable content in the films, as well as his borderline obsession with Hollywood. The Holy Spirit reveals the compromise John has made with the world system. So, he vows to make a major lifestyle change when he returns home.

The following Friday, his best friend calls him on the phone:

"Hey, man. We are still going to see that new movie coming out this weekend, right? The other guys said they are in."

"Ummm."

"What? Don't tell me you have other plans."

"It's not that," John says. "Actually, I was at that conference last weekend…and, well, the Lord really convicted me about the types of movies I have been watching."

"What do you mean?" his friend asks.

"I think I should be careful not to watch movies with profanity, violence and sexual scenes."

"Dude, we've been watching movies like that forever. It was never an issue before."

"It's just a commitment I made to the Lord."

"So what are you saying, that we are sinning?"

"I feel like this is a way that I need to honor God," John tries to explain.

"Really? What do you think, you are some kind of super Christian now?"

"I'm just trying to obey what I feel like God is telling me personally…"

This conversation could then go a few different directions. If John's friend genuinely cared about their friendship, not only would he be supportive, but he might even search his own heart to see if he needed to reconsider his own lifestyle choices. However, if that friend had no interest in truly pursuing the Lord, it would not be uncommon for him to try to pressure John to give up his convictions by giving him the, "Everyone in the church is doing it" speech. Or he might completely write him off as a fanatic and cut relational ties, leaving John to search for new friends who respect and share his convictions.

What took place in this situation between John and his best friend? In an effort to live the Crucified Lifestyle, John made a decision that clashed with the lifestyle of those around him. Even though he was not trying to call out compromise in his friend's life, his decision became a silent finger pointing at it. There is no way to keep this from happening; it is the natural consequence of the pursuit of holiness. This is why we need to choose in our hearts to live for God's opinion rather than man's. If John does not allow himself to die to the opinions of his friends, he may very well go back to the lifestyle of compromise from which the Lord was trying to help him escape. T. F. Tenney said it this way, "The closer you get to the cross, the smaller the crowd becomes."[14]

Everyone who endeavors to live the Crucified Lifestyle will be faced with situations on a regular basis in which a decision must be made: either fear man or fear God. The sooner we come to grips with this truth, the more prepared we will be to live out the cross-centered life.

# THE FEAR OF MAN AND THE PULPIT

Unfortunately, the fear of people has a crippling effect on many pulpits. In some churches, a distorted message is being proclaimed in an effort to please people. It teaches that we can choose to follow Christ and yet live for ourselves. This watered-down version of the Gospel is created by removing the offensive parts of following Christ, such as self-denial and cross-carrying, and instead focusing only on the benefits of discipleship. The message contains truth, but by omitting some of the less fashionable aspects of following Jesus, it becomes a truncated version of the Gospel. Essentially it is the equivalent of an Uncrucified Lifestyle.

Leonard Ravenhill once said, "We are preaching an acceptable Gospel today, making it as painless as we can."[15] At the very root of this kind of preaching is the fear of man. Paul warned Timothy about a time like ours:

> For the time will come when they will not endure sound doctrine, but according to their own desires, because they have itching ears, they will heap up for themselves teachers; and they will turn their ears away from the truth, and be turned aside to fables. **(2 Timothy 4:3-4)**

When people do not want sound doctrine, they will search for a church that gives them a message that will only encourage them and tell them what they want to hear. Ministers often feel the need to keep congregants in their churches. When people leave a church, they take their money and time, and the lack of resources can make ministry more difficult. In order to draw people and keep them in attendance, it is extremely tempting to soften the message ever so slightly. But what begins with a little compromise becomes an increasingly imbalanced and less biblical message. Sermons become pep talks and guidance on how to have a happier life, rather than a holier one. The church stops forming true disciples, and instead focuses on keeping church people complacent. Essentially, a minister who compromises the truth of the Gospel will actively put the people they serve to sleep spiritually.

The more watered-down the messages, the more difficult it becomes to go back to preaching the full Gospel. Some pastors repent and choose to return to preaching the truth, willing to risk losing members of their congregation for the sake of a clear conscience. Others continue to be driven by the fear of man and refuse to preach any sermon that might be deemed offensive.

The reality is that true believers should be offended at a spiritual leader who does *not* give them the full counsel of God. That should be something that causes a stir in a church. Pastors should be having people come to them and say, "Please preach about sin and repentance. Please challenge me to live a holy life. I am drying up spiritually with your self-help messages." But this is often the opposite reaction of people in the church. Let this be an encouragement to remember to pray for our spiritual leaders to stay true to the Word of God no matter what the cost! Be supportive of any man or woman of God who is doing their best to live and minister in the fear of the Lord.

The Apostle Paul also experienced opposition within the church, causing him to ask the question, "Have I now become your enemy by telling you the truth?"[16] However, he also provides an example for us of a man who never changed the message to please people. He stood his ground in the Lord, and the fruit of his ministry continues today because of his boldness. But this did not come without a spiritual fight.

Paul gives an interesting prayer request to the Ephesian church. He writes:

> Pray also for me, that whenever I speak, words may be given me so that I will fearlessly make known the mystery of the gospel, for which I am an ambassador in chains. Pray that I may declare it fearlessly, as I should. **(Ephesians 6:19-20 NIV)**

It is amazing that these are the words of the courageous and seemingly fearless apostle. With all the trials that he had endured, you might assume that he would not have any fear of preaching the Gospel. He had been stoned, shipwrecked, beaten and imprisoned during his ministry.[17] And yet, the fact that he requests prayer to preach fearlessly shows that he also was tempted to fear man. Paul's chief concern was, "God, don't let the fear of man keep me from sharing the Gospel as I should!"

## WHICH PATH WILL YOU CHOOSE?

When I was a child, I used to enjoy reading a unique style of books called "Choose Your Own Adventure." Every reader begins on the first page and continues until they hit a section break, where they are presented with two options. For example, at the end of a chapter from a mystery story, it might read:

If you would choose to run into the woods, go to page 195.
If you would choose to go into the house, go to page 210.

As you make decisions throughout the story, you create your own journey, as if you are the main character. Something about having control over the direction of the story appealed to me as a child.

In many ways, the format of Choose Your Own Adventure books provides a parallel to our lives. Throughout our life journey, we come to points of decision on a regular basis. Depending on what choice we make, we head in a certain direction. The pathway we walk is made up of a series of thousands of decisions that we have made. While there are some aspects of our lives that are outside of our control, how we reacted to those situations was still a part of choosing our own adventure.

Picture yourself standing at a crossroad. On one side, the pathway is a life in which the opinions of others are the most important thing to you. You choose to live under the burden of people-pleasing, always trying to make sure that nothing you do or say offends anyone, even when you know it is what the Lord desires. In essence, your life purpose is to make sure everyone likes you. At the end of your adventure, your epithet will read, "Crippled by the Fear of Man."

There is another path. This one is comprised of living according to God's opinion. It means choosing to live in the way prescribed by His Word and according to His Spirit. This path will bring you into conflict with others at times. Not everyone in the world—or even in the church—will understand or support your lifestyle. You may bear a stigma as a radical and be considered strange. Yet in the end, your epithet will read, "Crucified with Christ."

The second path represents the Crucified Lifestyle. It requires crucifixion to the fear of man, and obedience to God and His ways. If you were to die today, which one of these testimonies is closer to the truth? Would Heaven look down at your life and say that you truly lived the Crucified Lifestyle or that you were unwilling to follow Jesus on His terms because you focused on man's opinion? The choice belongs to each of us. History will one day tell which path we chose.

# SECTION THREE:

## A SURRENDERED LIFESTYLE

Having examined three incredible benefits afforded us by the Crucified Lifestyle, we will now switch our lens from the theme of victory to the theme of surrender. *Surrender* means, "to acknowledge defeat and by doing so put oneself in the power of an adversary."[1] It occurs in war when one nation overpowers another, and the weaker nation accepts defeat. In historical wars, a white flag has often been raised to signify surrender on the battlefield. The conquering nation is then given power to handle the opposing nation as it sees fit. The white flag cancels the surrendering nation's right to govern itself. Instead, that right is transferred to the nation to whom it had surrendered.

This illustration of two warring nations falls short because God is not an enemy of His children. However, serving Him is an assault on our self-life. Paul said, "The mind governed by the flesh is hostile to God; it does not submit to God's law, nor can it do so."[2] Walking in the fullness of relationship with Jesus involves raising a white flag of surrender to Him in our hearts. Discipleship requires that we forfeit control of our lives and submit ourselves to His rule and reign. He is supposed to be the One who oversees our lives, dictates our behavior and directs our paths.

The Crucified Lifestyle is synonymous with a Surrendered Lifestyle. In the following three chapters, we will discuss three important parts of our lives that must be surrendered to the Lordship of Christ: our personal rights, our plans and our finances.

"The only right a Christian has is the right to give up his rights."

-Oswald Chambers[1]

CHAPTER

# 6

## SURRENDERING OUR PERSONAL RIGHTS

*Crucified Christians Cease Demanding Their Own Way*

WESTERN CULTURE HAS A BORDERLINE obsession with the issue of rights. People in our society are in continual debate about what rights they believe should belong to all people, such as the right to free speech, the right to end an unwanted pregnancy, the right to medically assisted suicide and the right to vote. People make statements like, "I have the right to do what I want," or, "You don't have the right to do that to me." But what role do personal rights play in the lives of those who have entered into the lifestyle of the cross?

Jesus explained in Luke 9:23 that discipleship requires cross-carrying, which results in death to ourselves. When a criminal was carrying his crossbeam up the hill toward the crucifixion site, his personal rights were already stripped away from him. He was allowed no input into how he was treated. Rather, he was required to obey the instruction of the soldiers. A sentenced prisoner had no bartering rights. Even if he tried to make some kind of demand on the soldiers, they were under no obligation to comply, and his request would most likely fall on deaf ears. As A.W. Tozer put it:

> The man with a cross no longer controls his destiny; he lost control when he picked up his cross. That cross immediately became to him an all-absorbing interest, an overwhelming interference. No matter what he may desire to do, there is but one thing he can do; that is, move on toward the place of crucifixion.[2]

Dead people have no personal rights. No one argues about their rights being violated from the grave. Spiritually speaking, we too must daily die to our selfish ambitions and the desire to have our own way.

## THE LORDSHIP OF CHRIST

The concept of surrendering our rights is not popular in the Western church. However, it is necessary to address this topic if we desire to live the cross-life. Before we came to Christ, we lived with the preconceived notion that our lives were ours to live however we chose. That belief is a misconception because the Bible describes unbelievers as slaves to sin and the devil.[3] Nevertheless, the world teaches us the erroneous idea that we have the right to live however we desire, and that no one should ever be able to take that right away. However, when we accept Christ and enter His discipleship process, we must be willing to nail our so-called rights to the cross. A my-way-or-the-highway mentality is completely incongruent with the Crucified Lifestyle.

The discussion about a believer's personal rights can be boiled down to one critical question: "Is Jesus really the Lord of my life?" Repentance and spiritual rebirth necessitate a decision to live according to His ways. We begin to approach life with a completely different set of principles from the world. Our supposed personal rights must be forfeited in order to follow

Jesus according to His terms. Rather than having a selfish pre-occupation with our rights, we are to surrender them completely to the Lord.

When a person is born again, they are essentially saying, "Here is my life, Lord. It's yours to do with as you please. I'm giving you full control from this day forward." It is similar to a man who decides to join the military. There are certain freedoms that a soldier surrenders when dedicating his life to serving his country. While other citizens have the right to move to any community they choose, the soldier is given orders as to where he will live and how long he will spend at that destination. If it is time to be deployed to war, the country does not have to ask the soldier permission. They simply send him orders and he is expected to obey. Disobedience to those orders comes with consequences.

Essentially, the soldier who is enlisted in military service is saying, "I agree to serve my country and dedicate my life for this cause while I am enlisted. I surrender many of my personal rights for the sake of military service." This is the same type of agreement we are making with God when we choose to serve Him. As Paul wrote to Timothy, "You therefore must endure hardship as a good soldier of Jesus Christ. No one engaged in warfare entangles himself with the affairs of this life, that he may please him who enlisted him as a soldier."[4] The attitude of every disciple must be transformed from a self-pleasing attitude into one that seeks to please God.

We often talk about making Jesus Lord and Savior of our lives, but it seems that many want Jesus to be their Savior yet are not really interested in serving Him as Lord. They see their need to be forgiven of their sins, but they want the pardon without the responsibility. They want the promise of Heaven, without the need to surrender their lives on earth. The Lordship of Christ is more than a title. It is a recognition of His majesty and His authority that should cause us to throw ourselves at His feet in utter surrender. When we truly see ourselves in light of Him, this is the only proper response.

## WHO OCCUPIES THE THRONE?

Coming to Christ involves a change of loyalty. We no longer sit on the throne of our lives and make decisions that serve our best interests. Rather, we step off the throne and allow Jesus to reign as King. Our allegiance must change from serving ourselves to serving our new Master; we cannot have it both ways. Anything less is not biblical Christianity. The issue is one of submission to God's rightful authority. As we allow Him to reign in our lives, we begin to live in surrender to the Lord and His commands.

Take a family as an example. For a household to function smoothly, the parents need to be the ones occupying the seat of order and control. When children are allowed to take that place, chaos ensues. When parents rule their homes with love and understanding—and the children submit to their parents' authority—peace and order will dominate the home. It is the same for believers. When Christ is allowed to occupy the throne of our lives, everything falls into place, and we bear fruit. When we attempt to put self on the throne, chaos will follow. We were not created to be the rulers of our own lives. That desire is a result of the Fall, when mankind rebelled against the one true King. As Crucified Christians, having been forgiven of our rebellion and sin, we need to die to the desire to be in control, and instead submit our lives to Him. Tozer explains:

> In every Christian's heart there is a cross and a throne, and the Christian is on the throne till he puts himself on the cross; if he refuses the cross, he remains on the throne. Perhaps this is at the bottom of the backsliding and worldliness among gospel believers today. We want to be saved, but we insist that Christ do all the dying. No cross for us, no dethronement, no dying.[5]

Unfortunately, rather than make Christ the sole occupier of the throne, some professing Christians only desire to incorporate Him into their lives to ease their consciences. Jesus is not looking to be Lord over some of our lives. He is looking for a complete surrender to Him in every area. Hudson Taylor once said, "He is either Lord of all, or not Lord at all."[6] We all wrestle with complete submission to the Lord at times. However, when you look at the overall lifestyle of true believers, there will be clear evidence that Jesus' authority influences their decisions and character. There is only room on the throne for one person. Because God gives us a free will, we choose who will occupy that seat of authority.

## I SURRENDER ALL

Any believer can claim to be surrendered to Christ. In fact, most of us in the church can sing the chorus by heart:

I surrender all, I surrender all;
All to thee my blessed Savior,
I surrender all.[7]

These words sound beautiful when set to music and sung in harmony. Since 1896, people in churches have proclaimed these words boldly. But how many of us are living that song out in our daily lives? Surrender to Christ must be more than songs we sing on Sundays. It looks like a life laid down in submission to God's authority. Surrender is a day-by-day, moment-by-moment decision to obey Him. It is a lifestyle of continually saying "Yes" to His will.

Paul referred to this type of lifestyle as walking in the Spirit.[8] As we learn to live according to the Holy Spirit's desires—rather than our own— we will find ourselves surrendering our personal rights. Learning this kind of submission to the Lord is a lifelong process, but it is something that we should be displaying in increasing measure as we mature in our faith.

Dietrich Bonhoeffer spoke about surrender this way:

Only a man totally committed in discipleship can experience the meaning of the cross...When Christ calls a man, he bids him come and die...because only the man who is dead to his own will can follow Christ. In fact, every command of Jesus is a call to die, with all our affections and lusts.[9]

All of Christ's disciples must raise the white flag of surrender, die to our right to live according to our selfish desires and follow Him according to His terms. Rather than merely words from a song, when people look at us, they should see our very lives singing: "I Surrender All." It is this type of lifestyle that clearly demonstrates that a person has been to the cross of Calvary.

# JESUS' SUBMISSION TO GOD

As followers of Christ, we are to emulate His example. John said in his epistle that we ought to live as Jesus lived.[10] Our Savior forfeited His personal rights as a model for us. Think about the person of Jesus. Colossians 1:16 says, "For by Him all things were created that are in heaven and that are on earth, visible and invisible, whether thrones or dominions or principalities or powers. All things were created through Him and for Him." This is a striking truth. All things were created for and through Jesus. He is a member of the Trinity. He is the Creator. And yet, He came to earth and became one of us.

What did it look like for God Himself to walk the earth as a man? Not what many might expect. He did not come demanding the worship, glory and honor that is due to His name. It would be blasphemy for any human to accept worship. But Jesus had every right to receive it, being equal with God. Yet, the Scripture says that Jesus "did not consider equality with God something to be used to His own advantage."[11]

Have you ever considered what it was like for Jesus to be omnipotent, and yet set His divine power aside? What was it like to have all-knowledge, and yet allow Himself to be limited to the mental capacity of one of His creations? How could the omnipresent God be confined to the body of a human, even taking on the form of an infant? It is impossible for us to truly fathom what it meant for God to dwell among us. But even more incomprehensible, Scripture says that Jesus "made Himself nothing."[12]

At minimum Jesus had the right to be a powerful world ruler or an illustrious rich man. Yet, He chose to come to the earth as a servant. This is the great mystery of the incarnation of Christ. Jesus gave His disciples a powerful example by willingly relinquishing His personal rights. He lived a life of full surrender and perfect obedience to His Father, even submitting

Himself to the Cross.[13] And as His followers, we are to walk in His footsteps and set aside our personal rights for Him.

# WHAT RIGHTS ARE WE TO SURRENDER?

Now that we have established that our personal rights must be surrendered to live the Crucified Lifestyle, let us discuss more specifically what that entails. Examples of personal rights that are supposed to be surrendered are plentiful in the Scriptures. Missionary Elisabeth Elliot once searched through the Bible to determine which personal rights Christians must lay down. She published her findings in one of her newsletters.[14] Here are twelve of the rights she discovered:

**1. The Right to Take Revenge**

The world has the attitude that we have a right to repay those who mistreat us. Revenge is defined as, "harm done to someone as a punishment for harm that they have done to someone else."[15] The thing that motivates a vengeful person is the belief that being hurt gives us the right to give hurt in return. Retaliation is not only acceptable in our society, but even deemed as justice. We call it "settling the score" or "getting even." However, as believers, we are told to trust the Lord with justice. Rather than take revenge, we are to repay evil with love. Paul tells us plainly in Romans 12:19-20:

> Do not take revenge, my dear friends, but leave room for God's wrath, for it is written: "It is mine to avenge; I will repay," says the Lord. On the contrary: "If your enemy is hungry, feed him; if he is thirsty, give him something to drink. In doing this, you will heap burning coals on his head." (**NIV**)

Jesus displayed this attitude in the most vivid way when He chose to forgive the very ones who crucified Him on the cross.[16] He chose to put His attackers in God's hands rather than take revenge on them Himself.

## 2. The Right to Hate

Hatred is rampant in our world, especially when it is directed at those who we might consider enemies. You hear it in people's conversations and see it posted on social media. Yet Jesus tells us that believers are not only to forfeit the right to hate our enemies, but in addition, we must love and even pray for them. In the Sermon on the Mount, Jesus gives us practical advice about hatred, when He says:

> You have heard that it was said, 'You shall love your neighbor and hate your enemy.' But I say to you, love your enemies, bless those who curse you, do good to those who hate you, and pray for those who spitefully use you and persecute you…(**Matthew 5:43-44**)

There is no room for hatred in the heart of a Crucified Christian. That right has been hammered to the cross, and love is to be our response in every situation.

## 3. The Right to Be Served

The world operates on a hierarchy, where people who wield power expect to be catered to by those underneath them. This is contrary to the way that God's Kingdom operates. Jesus says that we must surrender our 'right' to be honored and served by others, even if we are in a position of power. In Mark 10, Jesus uses His own life as an example of humility despite the ordinary cultural practices:

> You know that those who are considered rulers over the Gentiles lord it over them, and their great ones exercise authority over them. Yet it shall not be so among you; but whoever desires to become great among you shall be your servant. And whoever of you desires to be first shall be slave of all. For even the Son of Man did not come to be served, but to serve, and to give His life a ransom for many. (**vss.42-45**)

Jesus gave His disciples an unforgettable lesson in serving others when He washed their feet in John 13. If the Lord of all the earth came and took the form of a servant, how much more should those who claim to be His disciples humbly serve the world around them rather than demanding service from them?

**4. The Right to Live by Our Own Rules**

Before we followed Christ, we lived our lives according to our own set of rules. We were the masters of our destinies and the ones who determined our morality and values. Many of us had parents and teachers who endeavored to instill certain character traits into our lives. But ultimately, we chose the rules that governed our decisions. The 'right' to be the lord of our own lives is forfeited at the cross. As disciples, we are called to submit ourselves to the Lord and His will. Jesus even says that obedience to His commands is proof of our love for Him:

> Anyone who loves me will obey my teaching. My Father will love them, and we will come to them and make our home with them. Anyone who does not love me will not obey my teaching. **(John 14:23-24 NIV)**

As the One who created us, Jesus retains the right to set the rules on how our lives are to be lived. He is expecting obedience and a sincere desire to live according to His Word from anyone who claims to be His disciple.

**5. The Right to Hold a Grudge**

Forgiveness is not optional for believers. We do not get to choose who is worthy of our forgiveness and withhold it from those who do not meet our criteria. In fact, Jesus teaches us that if we withhold forgiveness from others, our Heavenly Father will not forgive us.[17] He allows us no excuses for carrying a grudge or harboring bitterness against others. Paul continues with the same sentiment when he tells the Colossian church, "Bear with each other and forgive one another if any of you has a grievance against someone. Forgive as the Lord forgave you."[18] The Scriptures do not give us any examples in which embracing offense is acceptable.

To state it simply, no Christian has the 'right' to hold a grudge against anyone. Of course, this is easier said than put into practice, which is why we need the power of the Holy Spirit operating in our lives. We cannot forgive in our own strength, but only through His grace. However, despite the challenge of walking in forgiveness with those who hurt us, we never have the right to walk in unforgiveness toward others. Holding grudges may be common in the world but should be a practice that is absent from the church.

## 6. The Right to Fit Into Society

The desire to be accepted by others is an inherent trait of the human experience. Nobody wants to undergo rejection or become an outcast among their social peers. Some will go to incredible lengths to ensure that this never happens, even pretending to be someone that they are not in an effort to be accepted. We see this play out in the lives of many young people during their school years, desperately trying to fit into the "in crowd" so that they will not be seen as an outsider.

When we embark on the path of the Crucified Lifestyle, we must come to terms with the fact that we can no longer expect to fit into society. Our values are completely different than those of the world. The temptation to compromise what we believe in order to avoid rejection is ever-present. But as foreigners in this world, that is not an option.[19] Paul tells us plainly, "Do not be conformed to this world."[20] Therefore, Crucified Christians are non-conformists with the world around us. The pursuit of fitting in with the world must be abandoned for the sake of embracing the cross.

## 7. The Right to Do What Feels Good

"Do what you feel" is the mantra of our hedonistic culture. Society tells us that we ought to follow our hearts, and chase after whatever brings us pleasure. The advertising and entertainment industries push these values on us shamelessly. Regardless of what might be pleasurable to our flesh,

Crucified Christians live under the guidance of the Holy Spirit. Paul makes clear to the Galatians that the Spirit of God desires the opposite of what the flesh craves. They "are contrary to one another, so that you do not do the things that you wish."[21] Peter echoes this thought when he writes that Christians "do not live the rest of their earthly lives for evil human desires, but rather for the will of God."[22]

How something makes us feel can never be the filter through which we make our decisions. Instead, the Word of God and the leading of the Holy Spirit should be the governing forces of our lives. The reality is that we will not always feel like following Jesus. But we must discipline ourselves to live according to our faith, rather than our selfish desires. In fact, the fleshly nature that cries out to be catered to is instead to be put to death mercilessly.

### 8. The Right to Complain

The New Testament is clear that followers of Jesus must surrender their right to complain. Paul instructs the believers in Philippi, "Do all things without complaining,"[23] or you could say, "Don't do anything with complaining." Grumbling about our circumstances, no matter how difficult or unfair they may be, is incompatible with the Crucified Lifestyle.

While it may be an acceptable practice in the world to gripe about things we do not like, the Bible instructs us to, "Rejoice in the Lord always."[24] We are also told to have joy in trials.[25] When the apostles in Acts 5 experienced persecution for their faith, the Scripture tells us that they went along, "rejoicing that they were counted worthy to suffer shame for His name." (vs. 41) The Christian's perspective on difficulties in life should be completely different than the world's viewpoint. Therefore, we are to receive everything as if it is from God, without complaint. As John of the Cross wrote pointedly, "Whenever anything disagreeable or displeasing happens to you, remember Christ crucified and be silent."[26]

### 9. The Right to Put Self First

There is a philosophy that is common in the world called "Looking

117

out for Number One." In a dog-eat-dog society, we are often taught to do whatever is required to ensure our needs are taken care of, even if it means taking from others or cheating in some way. In the pursuit of worldly success, people often believe that the ends justify the means. As long as they achieve their desired goal—whether amassing wealth or attaining to a position of power—it does not matter who they need to trample on along the way.

Philippians 2:3-4 tells us, "Let nothing be done through selfish ambition or conceit, but in lowliness of mind let each esteem others better than himself. Let each of you look out not only for his own interests, but also for the interests of others." The truth of this Scripture is diametrically opposed to the way society teaches us to treat other people. Rather than viewing others as stepping stones to get what we want, we are to search for ways to serve them and honor them over ourselves. To live this way requires a continual death to our own selfish desires as we surrender our 'right' to elevate ourselves at the expense of others.

### 10. The Right to Express Our Sexuality in Ways That Are Contrary to the Ways of God

The Scriptures address sexual sin in multiple places in both the Old and New Testaments. One example is 1 Corinthians 6:18-20, which states:

> Flee sexual immorality. Every sin that a man does is outside the body, but he who commits sexual immorality sins against his own body. Or do you not know that your body is the temple of the Holy Spirit who is in you, whom you have from God, and you are not your own? For you were bought at a price; therefore glorify God in your body and in your spirit, which are God's.

The biblical message about human sexuality is that it is designed by God and is to be governed within His boundaries. Anything outside of that design (which is one man and one woman in a marriage covenant for a lifetime) is strictly forbidden. While many in society have the attitude that they should be able to freely indulge in sexual acts with whomever they choose, Christians forfeit the 'right' to do so.

In addition, Genesis 1:27 explains that "God created man in His own image; in the image of God He created him; male and female He created them." While the secular world throws around ideas about gender such as "gender fluidity" and "nonbinary gender identity," the Bible speaks about two distinct genders that God chooses and assigns for us at conception. Although the world may believe that humans have the right to choose their own gender, a believer is to allow the Word of God to shape their understanding of what it means to be a man or a woman.

## 11. The Right to Rebel Against Authority

Jesus walked the earth at a time when Israel was ruled by one of the world's harshest countries in history. Rome was known as a bloodthirsty and power-hungry nation. They treated the Jews with disdain and viewed themselves as the superior race. Besides the Romans, many of the Jewish rulers themselves were corrupt and immoral. Herod Antipas, for example, had John the Baptist imprisoned for calling out his immoral relationship with his brother's wife.[27] If any people group ever had the right to rebel against the corrupt authority over them, you would think it would be the Jews of Jesus' day.

What some find surprising about Jesus' ministry is that He never encouraged anyone to rebel against crooked leadership. In fact, His recorded teachings are mostly devoid of criticism against the government. Rather, He modeled and taught submission to authority.

Peter went on to write:

> Submit yourselves for the Lord's sake to every human authority: whether to the emperor, as the supreme authority, or to governors, who are sent by him to punish those who do wrong and to commend those who do right. For it is God's will that by doing good you should silence the ignorant talk of foolish people.
> **(1 Peter 2:13-15 NIV)**

Keep in mind that Peter is writing these words during the reign of the Emperor Nero, who was fiercely persecuting Christians and putting them to death. Clearly, Peter did not teach that we have the right to rebel against those in authority over us, regardless of how we are treated.

**12. The Right to End a Disappointing Marriage**

We live in a time period when divorce is so common, it no longer carries much of a stigma in our society. Broken homes have become the norm. Yet, the belief that "falling out of love" is a rightful excuse for divorce does not line up with the Scriptures. The Bible is clear that marriage is to be a lifetime commitment—through thick and thin—until one of the spouses passes on from this life. In the case of physical abuse or marital unfaithfulness, a separation or divorce may be warranted. However, even in these cases, if true repentance occurs, the spouse can choose to forgive and move toward reconciliation if possible. Jesus made this statement, which is just as controversial today as it would have been when He spoke it:

> Furthermore it has been said, 'Whoever divorces his wife, let him give her a certificate of divorce.' But I say to you that whoever divorces his wife for any reason except sexual immorality causes her to commit adultery; and whoever marries a woman who is divorced commits adultery. (**Matthew 5:31-32**)

The bottom line is that Crucified Believers who have entered the covenant of marriage are to live according to a different standard than the world. A biblical commitment to their spouses makes it necessary for Christians to surrender their 'right' to end a marriage due to disappointment or a change of emotions.

# DO CHRISTIANS MAINTAIN ANY RIGHTS?

It might seem overwhelming to discover all the personal rights that we are to surrender at the cross. In fact, there are many more than the

## SIX: SURRENDERING OUR PERSONAL RIGHTS

twelve listed above that could be discussed. However, there is a positive spin to each of the rights that we just examined. Our flesh will focus on all the rights that we must give up and accuse God of being harsh or unfair. However, by surrendering these personal rights, we have given up the need to:

1. Even the score with others through our own efforts
2. Harbor hatred and resentment in our hearts
3. Forfeit the blessing that comes from serving others
4. Live out the consequences of holding unbiblical values
5. Have damaged relationships and a hardened heart through unforgiveness
6. Live up to other people's expectations
7. Search for satisfaction in places that it cannot be found
8. Find the negative in every situation
9. Promote ourselves above others
10. Experience the destruction caused by sexual sin
11. Live in opposition to God-given authority
12. Walk through the pain of a failed marriage

When you think about the surrender of personal rights from this perspective, it no longer seems like such a sacrifice. The life of surrender actually positions us to live the best life we can on this earth!

I was teaching about surrendering our personal rights at a Bible school once and a student raised her hand and asked in exasperation, "From this lesson, it sounds like we just have to give everything up and keep nothing for ourselves. Do we even have any rights at all?" As I pondered that answer, I realized that the Bible does give us incredible rights as children of God. At the top of that list is John 1:12, which says, "But as many as received Him, to them He gave the right to become children of God, to those who believe in His name." Can you imagine that? Through our faith in Christ, God has given us the right to become His children! None of the personal rights that we have discussed in this chapter would be worth holding onto if it meant forfeiting that one. To become adopted into the family of God Almighty trumps any selfish right that we may be tempted to keep.

Included in that one right is a full package of benefits that come from surrendering to Christ. We have the right to expect God to meet our needs.[28] We have a right to pray and see the Lord answer our prayers.[29] We have the right to trust God to be true to His Word.[30] The Scriptures not only detail the personal rights we forfeit, but also the spiritual rights we gain as God's adopted children. What the cross has afforded us is truly remarkable!

## SELF OR CHRIST?

The issue of personal rights can all be boiled down to one question: Who will we truly live for, ourselves or the Lord? We can only serve one master. As Steve Gallagher accurately states:

> The reason many Christians cringe when they are asked to sacrifice for the sake of others is that nothing has happened within them to compel them to get outside of themselves. They see carrying a cross as an uninvited intrusion upon their lives. In their heart of hearts, their true devotion is reserved for the world system that caters to their flesh.
>
> The fundamental difference between a true and false believer lies in the question of loyalty. Is he devoted to Christ or to himself? When it comes right down to it, is he going to look out for 'number one' or will his primary loyalties be to Christ? Will he do his own will or that of God? Will he love Self or will he love the Lord? Being born again means the person is converted from a Self-centered existence to one which is becoming increasingly Christ-centered.

Such people do not want to deny Self; they want to live for Self. They do not want to say *no* to the flesh; they want to say *yes* to it. They do not want to pick up their cross; they want to avoid it... Where did they get the idea that they could live for Self, disdain the Cross and still claim to be followers of Christ?[31]

Jesus promises a rich, abundant life to those who follow Him. However, access to that life is contingent on our level of surrender. The Crucified Lifestyle demands that we surrender our personal rights to the Lord. As we do so, we will discover a renewed peace, joy and freedom in our relationship with God.

The next chapter will deal with another area of surrender with which we must all come to grips: the surrender of our plans.

"I find that doing of the will of God leaves me no time for disputing about His plans."

-George MacDonald[1]

# CHAPTER

# 7

## SURRENDERING OUR PLANS

*Crucified Christians Endeavor to Fulfill
God's Purpose for their Lives*

*"What do you want to be when you grow up?"*

That is a question that all children have been asked at least once. Adults like to inspire the next generation to dream about their future. Many of us grew up with parents, teachers and other key figures in our lives who instilled in us the belief that we can become whatever we desire. And while those childhood dreams often change as we progress through life, the ability to dream about the future is something that never leaves us.

Having the capacity to make intentional plans is a quality that we share with God as humans made in His image. No other living creature is capable of planning for its long-term future. While animals operate by instincts according to their design, the ability to make intellectual plans is a characteristic unique to humanity. Not only can we dream about the future, but we are then able to take practical steps to achieve our goals. Whether our plans involve pursuing education and a career, getting married and starting a family, amassing wealth, or making an impact in the world, for most of us, dreaming about the future is a very important element of our lives here on earth. It provides us with a sense of purpose and accomplishment when we realize our goals.

The challenge with our innate ability to dream and plan is that it gives us the impression that we can control our future. Although our actions help determine the direction of our lives (such as hard work, pursuing education and seeking counsel), there are many aspects completely out of our control. And beyond that reality, Crucified Christians must make room for the will of God and be willing to surrender our plans when they do not line up with His.

## HIS PLAN OR OURS?

Before we were born again, our dreams were built upon natural criteria. We made our decisions based on our personal giftings, the potential for making money, our own desires or sometimes other people's desires for us. We lived as if we were the masters of our own destiny. We were the ones who determined what we wanted out of life. But all that is supposed to change when we encounter the cross.

When we enter a relationship with God through Christ, it is no longer acceptable to simply pursue what is in our hearts without first consulting the Lord about it. The question is no longer, "What do I want to do?" but "What do *You* want me to do?" This is not to say that the answer to those two questions will always be different. Certainly, the Lord may have placed a particular dream in our hearts for His purposes. However, our motivation must change from doing what we want, to living out our plans for the glory of God. Essentially, we surrendered the right to determine our own future when we bowed our knee at the cross. Our life now belongs to the Lord and He can do with us as He wishes.

Proverbs 16:3 tells us, "Commit to the Lord whatever you do, and he will establish your plans." (NIV) Here the Bible describes a life of submission to God's leading. The problem is that many Christians are not willing to fully trust the Lord with their futures. They are afraid of what it might cost if they truly obeyed Him. What if He asked them to do something drastic or travel to a remote country to spread the Gospel? In fear, sometimes they continue to live their lives according to their own plans, while maintaining the outward appearance of a fully committed Christian life.

Consider the experience of Jesus' original twelve disciples. Choosing to follow Christ was not a one-time decision that they made in a church service. Making the decision to follow the Rabbi meant a radical alteration of their lifestyles, including walking away from their careers. Look at the following passages that describe the calling of five disciples:

> And Jesus, walking by the Sea of Galilee, saw two brothers, Simon called Peter, and Andrew his brother, casting a net into the sea; for they were fishermen. Then He said to them, "Follow Me, and I will make you fishers of men." They immediately left their nets and followed Him. Going on from there, He saw two other brothers, James the son of Zebedee, and John his brother, in the boat with Zebedee their father, mending their nets. He called them, and immediately they left the boat and their father, and followed Him. **(Matthew 4:18-22)**

> As Jesus passed on from there, He saw a man named Matthew sitting at the tax office. And He said to him, "Follow Me." So he arose and followed Him. **(Matthew 9:9)**

These passages are both fascinating and convicting. With just a few words from our Savior, these men walked away from what was most likely the only career they had ever known to follow Jesus. They were willing to surrender their livelihoods in order to follow the Teacher, whom they hardly knew at that time, into an uncertain future. Should we not be willing to do the same as modern-day disciples?

Romans 12 tells us that we are to present our bodies to the Lord as a living sacrifice. (vs. 1) The imagery of this verse illustrates laying our lives on the altar and allowing the Lord to use us for His glory alone. This might be a terrifying thought for those who desire to control their own destiny. But it is liberating for the one who truly wants to be used as an instrument in the hands of the Lord. The place of greatest peace, joy and fruitfulness will always be in God's will. The Crucified Lifestyle is one in which we lay ourselves at the feet of Jesus and say, "I'll do whatever you ask me to do and go wherever you ask me to go."

## KNOWING THE LORD'S WILL

One question that is commonly asked by believers is, "How do I discern the will of the Lord for my life?" In his epistle, James talks about making room for the will of God in our future plans. He says:

> Come now, you who say, "Today or tomorrow we will go to such and such a city, spend a year there, buy and sell, and make a profit"; whereas you do not know what will happen tomorrow. For what is your life? It is even a vapor that appears for a little time and then vanishes away. Instead you ought to say, "If the Lord wills, we shall live and do this or that." **(James 4:13-15)**

This passage is not telling us that we should not make plans. In fact, there are a number of other Scriptures that encourage us to do so.[2] Planning is not only wise, but it is integral to properly stewarding the life the Lord gave us. However, it is critical that we make room in our plans for the will of God. Following His leading is the most important aspect of our future. He knows which way we should go, and also warns us of the danger of going our own way. That is why Proverbs 14:12 says, "There is a way that seems right to a man, but its end is the way of death." God—who can see the end from the beginning—is able to lead us on a path that will benefit our lives and His Kingdom, even if we do not fully understand where He is taking us. Following Jesus requires that we put our faith in His wisdom and guidance.

Discipleship involves a desire to discover the Lord's will for our lives. When we come to Christ, it is natural for us to ask the question, "What do you want me to do for you, Lord?" Following the will of God is an amazing adventure, because it gives our lives an eternal purpose. Where once we had only natural goals in mind, now we are able to make an eternal impact in the lives of people around us. What an amazing privilege we have!

When we discuss God's will for our lives, there are two primary components to consider:

### *General will*

There is a general aspect of God's will that is revealed in the Scriptures which applies to all believers. For example:

- We are all called to praise and worship the Lord (**Psalm 100**)
- We are all called to share our faith (**1 Peter 3:15**)
- We are all called to pray (**Philippians 4:6**)
- We are all called to glorify God (**1 Corinthians 10:31**)
- We are all called to walk in purity (**1 Thessalonians 4:3**)
- We are all called to be holy (**1 Peter 1:15-16**)
- We are all called to be generous (**2 Corinthians 9:11**)
- We are all called to give thanks (**1 Thessalonians 5:18**)
- We are all called to do good works (**1 Peter 2:15**)

The Scriptures are filled with examples like these of the general will of God. None of these require any confirmation from the Lord to do them; He has already made His will clear for us in His Word. All of us have a responsibility to learn the Lord's general will for His children and then apply it to our lives. This is an important aspect of studying the Scriptures. Through God's Word, we discover and develop the proper motives, actions and attitudes of a Christ-follower.

*Specific will*

God will also call people to specific tasks and service that do not apply to all Christians. Every human was created uniquely for a purpose. Psalm 139 describes us as fearfully and wonderfully made. (vs. 14) Our Creator did not use a cookie-cutter when He fashioned us. Instead, He designed our DNA in such a way that no two fingerprints match. We each have different personalities, talents, gifts, backgrounds, abilities and experiences. And God did this intentionally so that we could bring Him glory through our individuality.

In his first letter to the Corinthians, Paul talks about the unique function of different members of the body of Christ. He describes it this way:

> If the whole body were an eye, where would be the hearing? If the whole were hearing, where would be the smelling? But now God has set the members, each one of them, in the body just as He pleased. And if they were all one member, where would the body be?[3]

We see in this passage that one person is not supposed to do everything. We each function differently according to our God-given design. In the Body of Christ, we each have an individual path to take as we endeavor to follow the Lord's specific will for our lives. He might call someone with the talent to sing and play instruments to lead worship. Another may be called to work with the homeless. One may be called to work in the marketplace while another is called to stay home and raise her children. Each person's specific path is unique, and we glorify the Lord when we walk in His specific calling.

Getting overly focused on walking a particular pathway can become unhealthy. Some Christians take this principle to the extreme and become fearful that they are constantly stepping out of God's will; questioning every move that they make. The Lord does not want us to live in this kind of fear. He is able to guide us by His Spirit and let us know when we need to change direction or reevaluate our plans. I fully believe that He will direct the path

## SEVEN: SURRENDERING OUR PLANS

of the believer who truly desires to serve Him. His specific will should be an exciting adventure to discover, not a heavy burden for us to bear.

While we all share the same general calling, the specific will of God for our lives will differ—and sometimes change—as we pass through various seasons of life. But both of these aspects of God's will are important for every believer to discover through prayer. Simply going through life without ever asking the Lord for direction has the potential to set a person on a path that will minimize their usefulness for the Kingdom of God and could even lead into destructive situations.

## MY BIG DREAM

Taking up our crosses according to Jesus' discipleship requirement may include dying to our own version of our dreams. As an illustration of the danger of pursuing dreams with unrealistic expectations and wrong motives, I want to share some difficult lessons that I learned first-hand.

Shortly after I gave my life to Christ in a Teen Challenge rehabilitation center,* I can remember sitting in my counselor's office. I was a brand-new believer, full of zeal for the Lord, and eager to live out His new plan for my life. The counselor asked me the question, "What are your dreams?"

I took a moment to ponder the question. As a young boy, I had always loved to make music. Writing lyrics and poetry was a skill that came naturally. I grew up dreaming that I would one day be on stage, singing songs with thousands of people echoing the words I had written. Throughout my teenage years, I learned to play guitar and keyboard and continued to write music. Then—in high school—I began to write rap songs and found out I had talent in that area as well. This was before my conversion, so my music up to that point was very worldly, filled with anger, pain and violence. But I loved making music and dreamed of success in the music industry. These were the thoughts that went through my mind as my counselor asked that question. So, I answered, "I want to be a successful musician."

His encouragement to me was, "Whatever you dream, dream big. God has big plans for you. Don't picture yourself doing small things for God; dream really big dreams!" Looking back, I appreciate the heart behind

---
*My full story is recorded in my first book, Pile of Masks.

his exhortation. He simply wanted to encourage me to believe God for great things in my life without limitations. However, taking his advice and applying it to my musical aspirations would set me on a destructive path that would eventually lead me away from the Lord.

Soon after the conversation, I began to write rap music with an evangelistic, Christ-centered focus. I wrote lyrics for an album and began to make plans to record it. I remember a Christian brother telling me, "God is going to make you famous, so you can make Him famous." Many people were equally encouraging when they saw the talent in my life. It was not uncommon for someone to say, "The Lord has a big plan for you." And I took what they said to heart.

As I continued to write and record music, doors opened to minister in churches, youth groups, music festivals, outreaches and other venues. As I saw how people responded and the lives that were impacted by my testimony, I believed that I had found the Lord's specific will for my life. In an effort to be a good steward of my talent, I made it a point to excel in my craft. I poured all my time, energy and resources into recording, writing and performing music. Becoming the best Christian musician became the all-consuming pursuit of my life. My desire to minister with excellence for the Lord may have been noble. However, without realizing it, my dream of success in the music industry became more about me than about serving Him.

## BUILDING THE WRONG KINGDOM

I cannot point to a specific day or even time period when my aspirations became idolatrous. But over time, my music ministry had become primarily a means to fulfill my childhood dreams. It was a subtle shift, and I did not even realize it was happening. But looking back, it is obvious that I had begun to try to build the kingdom of Me, rather than the Kingdom of God.

Increasing tension began to form as I looked for the "big break" that I believed the Lord was going to use to launch me into the public eye. I was so convinced of this that I expected at any time it was going to happen. Every time a new door would open, I thought, "Here it goes. This is when my music is going to explode!" But then, nothing would come of it. I had a couple of opportunities to perform in front of significant crowds, but it never seemed to amount to anything more. I became frustrated because I felt like the Lord was holding me back from my dream.

It was at this time that my wife and I met and began making plans for our future. She felt a call to be a missionary and I had also developed a heart for overseas ministry when I had gone on a missions trip. When we discussed the future, I stubbornly refused to entertain the thought that maybe the Lord was not going to make me a successful Christian musician. I could not see how my dream was going to fit into our plans to become missionaries. While I was not willing to admit it at the time, our future aspirations did not line up. It felt like we were trying to fit a square peg into a round hole.

Eventually, we made plans to pursue a career in full-time overseas missions. During this season, I remember crying out to God, asking why my music was not taking off the way I had planned. Rather than being open to consider that the Lord might have had a different plan for me, I grew bitter at Him. I rejected the notion that I might have made music into an idol. Instead, I dug in my heels, determined to make the dream happen in my own strength.

This became a huge stumbling block in my relationship with the Lord. I stopped believing that He was a good Father with my best interest in mind, and started seeing Him as cruel, hard and distant. It seemed that the harder I pursued my musical aspirations, the further away the possibility grew. I ended up with a bitter spirit and the issue was unresolved for several years as I sunk deeply into sin and pride while in ministry. But in His mercy, the Lord led me to Pure Life Ministries, where He brought me out of that dark spiritual place through nine months of repentance and restoration.

Even during that season, I was getting new inspiration for music. I was fully convinced that if I could record one more album, it would give me the best chance at getting noticed, and this time I could do it with the right heart. But after much internal wrestling, I realized I needed to lay the dream at the Lord's feet and allow Him to guide my future. And the result has been an incredible adventure with God that is beyond my wildest dreams, even though it looks nothing like what I had originally expected with my limited perspective of my future.

## GUARDRAILS FOR DREAMING

This experience taught me about the need to fully surrender my future to the Lord. As I look back over those difficult years, I see two warning signs that should have caused me to step back and evaluate what was taking place in my heart.

Picture a guardrail that is installed along the side of a highway going up a mountain. The purpose of guardrails is to keep vehicles safely on the road. If the guardrail was not there, it would be much easier to accidentally get too close to the edge and go off the side of the mountain. The following are two spiritual guardrails to help us ensure that we are keeping our dreams and plans in their proper Kingdom perspective.

**Guardrail #1: Expectation**

Following the Lord will not always look the way that we expect. In fact, it rarely looks anything like the pictures we conjure up in our imaginations. If our future expectations are too narrow, we run the risk of getting disillusioned in our walk with God. His plans are not guaranteed to line up with our own. However, they are always going to be exponentially better! The most fulfilling place that we can be in our lives is in God's will and the most miserable place is outside of it. If we are too rigid in our expectations of the future, we open the door for disappointment.

This was true in my own life. I began my ministry with specific expectations. I had a preconceived notion of how I believed the Lord was going to use me, and I was not willing to be flexible. When He did not meet my unrealistic expectations, disappointment set in. I began to believe that I could never be happy unless I had my dream fulfilled in the rigid way I expected.

If we are willing to serve the Lord in any way that He chooses, then we can avoid the pain of disappointment. After all, if you desire to serve the Lord without any expectations, you cannot be let down. As difficult as it can be to relinquish control of our lives, in actuality, it is liberating. We can leave our future in God's hands and trust Him to lead us. It sets us free from having to understand every detail and we can simply take our hands off the steering wheel of our lives and let Him have control. The Crucified Lifestyle demands flexibility and a willingness to follow the Lord even when it does not make sense or takes us somewhere in life we did not expect.

### *Guardrail #2: Motivation*

The world has its own system of promotion, which is predicated on "making a name for yourself." We see this mentality all around us. Politicians will attack one another and try to uncover scandalous information in order to sink their opponent. Businessmen will use other people to fight their way to the top of the corporate ladder. Often, corruption is a part of a person's climb to success. They are willing to lie, cheat and steal to increase their popularity and power. In order to make themselves look better, they need to make others look worse. Celebrities are often openly arrogant and self-promoting. The world's philosophy is, "Do whatever it takes to make it to the top."

Unfortunately, the same type of celebrity mindset can exist in the Christian world. We elevate people based on their talents, often at the expense of their character. Self-promotion exists in Christian industries and even in the pulpit. Many ministers move from one church to another in an attempt to gain prestige and increase the size of their congregations. The pursuit of money, influence and accolades can easily replace the pursuit of God's presence, power and pleasure.

Jesus never told us that we should strive to be Christian celebrities. Nor did He encourage His followers to make a name for themselves. In fact, He taught the exact opposite attitude. He frequently warned us about the desire to elevate ourselves. On one occasion, when He saw people choosing seats of honor at a feast, He encouraged His followers to take the seat of least importance. He drives His main point home by saying, "For whoever exalts himself will be humbled, and he who humbles himself will be exalted."[4] Jesus encourages the type of attitude that is humble and self-effacing. While the disciples were constantly trying to fight their way to the top,[5] Jesus was trying to help them understand the way that the Kingdom of God works. Serving Jesus is all about building His Kingdom rather than our own.

Servanthood—although very attractive to the Lord—is simply not trendy in the church. Servants do not get much attention because they are often not out in front of people. Rather, servanthood requires a willingness to serve without recognition. It is much easier in the church to find someone willing to sing a solo than it is to change diapers in the nursery. That is just the reality of Western church culture today.

When we are serving Christ out of a pure heart—without selfish motives—it does not matter if we are noticed or exalted in the eyes of other people. Part of the self-denial of discipleship may involve denying ourselves fame, praise or reputation. This does not mean that God will not allow us to be exalted at times. However, that should never be our goal or motivation. If we live for His glory alone, failing to receive the recognition of man will not leave us feeling disillusioned.

## EVALUATING OUR DREAMS

Surrendering our plans to the Lord is not meant to discourage God-given dreams. When we have a dream that we know is from the Lord, we should hold onto it at all costs. Just like Joseph's brothers, who hated him for his dream,[6] we will encounter people in our lives who will hate ours as well. It seems that the biggest persecutors of God-given dreams are those who never fulfilled their own. Some Christians will testify to the fact that they had a calling from God to do something specific, but they resisted. Some of them finally repent and choose to pursue the Lord's will, but others go to their grave without ever having reached their full potential in the Lord. Having a dream from the Lord is a wonderful gift, but we need to take the time to filter our dreams through the following questions:

- Is this something that God wants me to do?

- Do I have unrealistic expectations about what my future looks like?
- Is the motivation of my heart in the right place?
- Whose glory am I truly seeking by pursuing this dream?

While I was chasing after my musical aspirations, I would never have verbalized that it was self-serving. I was deceived to believe it was all about Jesus and that I had no desire to be in the limelight. But at some point, the yearning to be known and praised outgrew my desire to glorify the Lord. The reality is that—whether I had the talent to do it or not—becoming famous would have completely destroyed my life. I did not have the character or the maturity to handle bigger opportunities, when even the smallest ones caused me to become filled with pride. Today, I am extremely grateful to the Lord for preventing me from having what I thought I wanted. And He has released me into His plan for my life, where I have found fruitfulness and fulfillment in serving Him.

## LAYING OUR FUTURE ON THE ALTAR

One of the most difficult areas for many people to surrender to the Lord is their future. Many times, our identities are intertwined with our plans. Some people spend large amounts of time and money pursuing a certain career or goal. It becomes more than something they want to do; it becomes who they believe they are. They spend so much time dreaming about it that their entire perception of themselves is intricately wrapped up in their plans. So, asking the Lord if He has a different plan can be frightening because He might say "Yes." But this is a crucial part of living the Crucified Lifestyle.

Recall the story of Abraham and Isaac in Genesis 22. The story begins with the Lord asking Abraham to offer Isaac as a sacrifice to the Lord. While any person would struggle to obey a command like that, it is important to also note that Isaac was the child that God had promised to Abraham and Sarah in their old age.[7] Sarah had conceived through a supernatural miracle. And they had to wait twenty-five years to see the promise come to pass.

Isaac was symbolic of the fulfillment of God's dream for Abraham. He had promised to make a great nation out of him.[8] And that promise was contingent on this son that the Lord was asking Abraham to sacrifice. The most remarkable part of the story is that Scripture records:

> So Abraham rose early in the morning and saddled his donkey, and took two of his young men with him, and Isaac his son; and he split the wood for the burnt offering, and arose and went to the place of which God had told him.[9]

In a radical act of faith, Abraham was willing to literally put his future plans on the altar. When Abraham was just about to sacrifice Isaac, the Lord intervened and said, "Now I know that you fear God, since you have not withheld your son, your only son, from Me."[10] Isaac is a vivid illustration of something good in our lives that the Lord may ask us to sacrifice. Of course, in this story, God ended up allowing Abraham to keep his son, Isaac. But in our case, maybe the Lord wants us to leave our Isaac on the altar, so that He can accomplish His will for our lives instead.

As we bring this chapter to a close, perhaps it would do us all well to take a moment and consider the question: Do I have any dreams or plans that I have not taken the time to surrender to the Lord? Am I holding onto my future? Am I building His Kingdom or my own? We need to be willing to lay our futures at His feet and say, "Lord, I'm laying my plans down at the cross. I give you my life. I want to live the life *you* want me to live. I give you my desires and ask you to give me yours." He will certainly respond to the sincere cry of our hearts to live according to His will for our lives.

There is yet one more area of surrender that we must discuss in relation to the Crucified Lifestyle and that is the surrender of our finances.

"Money is really worth no more than as it can be used to accomplish the Lord's work. Life is worth as much as it is spent for the Lord's service."

-George Muller[1]

## CHAPTER

# 8

## SURRENDERING OUR FINANCES

*Crucified Christians Steward Their Resources
According to Biblical Principles*

THE CRUCIFIED LIFESTYLE PROVIDES FREQUENT opportunities for our faith to be tested. This life demands that we put our trust in a God that we cannot see, and believe His Word, even when it goes against our own reasoning. To surrender our personal rights, we must place our complete confidence in His ways rather than our own. To surrender our plans, we need to trust the Lord to guide us into His will. The third area of surrender is one in which our trust in God must also be tested, perhaps in a more tangible way than any other. In this chapter, we will examine the need for Jesus' disciples to fully surrender their finances to the Lord.

# MONEY AND THE CHRISTIAN LIFE

In the church world, ministers choose to handle the subject of finances in a variety of ways. Some refuse to broach the topic for fear of offending their congregants. Others give extensive teachings on giving while taking up their weekly offering. And a broad spectrum of methods exists between these two extremes. Regardless of one's opinion on how a church should or should not address the subject, the Word of God sheds much light on how we are to handle finances individually as children of God.

Money is a necessary part of life in most modern civilizations. Doing business and conducting affairs in society requires making use of the monetary system. Because of the greed and deceit that is often attached to wealth, some believers view it as evil. However, money itself is nothing more than a tool; it has no intrinsic moral value. The Bible informs us that the love of money is the root of all evil.[2] That is a strong warning, so we would do well to safeguard this area of our lives. But it is the lust for money that is sinful and opens the door for wickedness to enter our hearts, not the currency itself.

If you investigate the Scriptures for teaching on finances from God's perspective, you might be surprised at how often the topic is addressed. Throughout the Old and New Testaments, the Holy Spirit did not shy away from communicating godly standards for a believer's relationship to money. The way that we handle this aspect of our lives speaks volumes about what is in our hearts. Jesus said it plainly, "For where your treasure is, there your heart will be also."[3] For this reason, total surrender to the Lord must always include our finances. If we truly want to enter more fully into the cross-centered life, we need to be willing to crucify our wallets, so to speak.

# FINANCES AND THE EARLY CHURCH

When the Book of Acts describes the community of the early church, it provides us with insight into the way they handled their money and possessions. Luke records the following two descriptions:

Now all who believed were together, and had all things in common, and sold their possessions and goods, and divided them among all, as anyone had need. **(Acts 2:44-45)**

Now the multitude of those who believed were of one heart and one soul; neither did anyone say that any of the things he possessed was his own, but they had all things in common…Nor was there anyone among them who lacked; for all who were possessors of lands or houses sold them, and brought the proceeds of the things that were sold, and laid them at the apostles' feet; and they distributed to each as anyone had need. **(Acts 4:32-35)**

I find it intriguing that Luke goes into detail twice about the attitude of these early believers toward their possessions. It seems that the Scriptures are trying to teach us that part of the repentance process experienced by these new believers included a shift in their perspective on money. The early church quickly realized that their belongings were not something to selfishly hoard. In Western society, where the focus is often placed on amassing wealth and possessions, this type of communal sharing might seem unfair and unnecessary. We live in a culture that views a person's assets as theirs to do with as they please. But the early church clearly had a different opinion.

The way that the first century Christians surrendered their finances should challenge modern day believers to ask if our own bank statements reflect the Crucified Lifestyle we claim to live. While the same communal lifestyle may not apply to us, the principle of using our finances to be generous towards others certainly should. When we examine the way we store and spend our treasure, do we see the cross? Or do we find more evidence that our lifestyles are designed around our own enjoyment, security and happiness? This is the reason that the Bible has so much to say about money. Wealth is more of a thermometer of our trust in God than it is a sign of our affluence and power in the world. If someone claims to love the Lord and have a passion for His Kingdom, you should be able to see evidence of it in the way they handle their assets. We may not share everything communally with other believers, as the early church did.

However, like the believers in the book of Acts, the way that we handle our finances should be completely different than those who do not name Christ as Savior.

## BIBLICAL STEWARDSHIP

As believers, our perception about finances needs to be founded upon Scriptural principles. Rather than viewing our money as our own to use as we please, the biblical way to handle our finances is through the principle of stewardship. A steward is "a person who manages another's property or financial affairs."[4] Stewards are not the owners of the assets that they manage, therefore every financial decision must be made with the owner in mind. "What would the owner want me to do in this situation? How can I best invest his resources to bring about the most desirable result?" These are the kinds of questions that stewards use as a filter for making financial decisions. And it is a perfect description of how we should approach our finances as Crucified Christians.

Paul instructed Timothy about how Christians should treat money:

> Command those who are rich in this present age not to be haughty, nor to trust in uncertain riches but in the living God, who gives us richly all things to enjoy. (**1 Timothy 6:17**)

Here, Paul addresses the human tendency to put our trust mistakenly in our resources rather than in the Lord. This is especially tempting when we are in a season of abundance. It is often our impulse to place our trust in our careers, retirement, social status or even our own ability to create wealth without realizing it. But the Bible teaches that every good gift comes from God.[5] It also reminds us that He is the One who gives us the ability to create wealth.[6] To place our trust in anything other than our Creator is to misplace our trust. As the Psalmist says in Psalm 62:10, "If riches increase, do not set your heart on them." Paul continues:

> Let them do good, that they be rich in good works, ready to give,

willing to share, storing up for themselves a good foundation for the time to come, that they may lay hold on eternal life. **(1 Timothy 6:18-19)**

This Scripture explains that those who have wealth need to use it for the benefit of others, which will result in eternal treasure. Paul is encouraging us to not regard money from a natural viewpoint—as the world does—but to look at it from a spiritual perspective. As Jesus commanded, "Lay up for yourselves treasures in heaven, where neither moth nor rust destroys and where thieves do not break in and steal."[7] Any perceived value in the resources that we have in this life should be filtered through this Kingdom mindset.

We see in Paul's admonition to Timothy that it is not sinful to be rich, but there is a temptation for those who are wealthy to become greedy and forget about God. Therefore, he prescribes generosity and an eternal perspective to those who are blessed with riches. The Book of Proverbs provides us with the following prayer on financial contentment:

Give me neither poverty nor riches—Feed me with the food allotted to me; Lest I be full and deny You, And say, "Who is the LORD?" Or lest I be poor and steal, and profane the name of my God. **(Proverbs 30:8-9)**

God is the only one who knows how much wealth each of us can handle. We should exercise wisdom and pray that He will provide us with enough to meet our needs and be generous toward others. If we are not careful, the pursuit of riches can become an obstacle in our dependence on God.

Crucified Christians understand that everything they have comes from the Lord, and they are only caretakers of what He entrusts to them. Stewarding the Lord's resources does not mean that it is wrong to spend money on ourselves. However, if we never take the time to learn how to handle money the way the Lord desires, we will not only walk in disobedience, but also prevent the blessing of the Lord from flowing in our lives. With that in mind, let us examine some basic biblical principles on financial stewardship.

## TITHING

A study on biblical finances will quickly uncover the concept of tithing. The word *tithe* in Hebrew is *ma'ser* and literally means, "a tenth part."[8] The first example of this principle is found in the story of Abram, when he meets the mysterious king of Salem named Melchizedek. Genesis 14 tells us that this king brought bread and wine to Abram after his victory against the four kings who had captured Lot. And verse 20 simply states, "Then Abram gave him a tenth of everything," speaking of the spoils of war. We are not told that Abram was commanded to do so. It seems that he did this of his own volition.

Another example of tithing comes from Abraham's grandson, Jacob, in Genesis 28. This occurs shortly after he receives a prophetic dream and confirmation of God's covenant with him. When Jacob awakens, he makes a conditional vow to the Lord that he will give Him a tenth of everything he has if the Lord would bless him.[9] Both of these examples occurred before the Lord required it of the Israelites. It is notable that the *principle* of tithing was introduced into the biblical narrative before the *precept* from the Law was given.

## TITHING IN THE MOSAIC LAW

Long after these accounts, when God revealed the Law to the nation of Israel, He included this practice in the way that they were to steward their possessions:

> And all the tithe of the land, whether of the seed of the land or of the fruit of the tree, is the Lord's. It is holy to the Lord…And concerning the tithe of the herd or the flock, of whatever passes under the rod, the tenth one shall be holy to the Lord. (**Leviticus 27:30-32**)

It almost seems as if the Lord took what Abraham did for Melchizedek and what Jacob committed to the Lord and turned it into a standard practice for the whole nation of Israel. And He had an intentional reason for incorporating this practice. Tithing was based on the principle that a tenth of everything the land produced belonged to God. Through this stewardship commandment, the Lord was conditioning the minds of His people to view everything they received through the filter of tithing. He would bless them and provide one hundred percent of their needs, but He expected them to give ten percent back to Him.

The tithe had a practical purpose as well. Out of the twelve tribes of Israel, the Lord selected Levi to be the priesthood for the nation. Every other tribe received a portion of the land as an inheritance, but the Levites were not supplied with any land. The way that the Lord provided for the tribe of Levi was through the tithe:

> I give to the Levites all the tithes in Israel as their inheritance in return for the work they do while serving at the tent of meeting. This is a lasting ordinance for the generations to come. They will receive no inheritance among the Israelites. (**Numbers 18:21, 23 NIV**)

This was the financial system that the Lord Himself instituted for His people. They were to return to the Lord ten percent of their increase, and He would use it to provide for the priesthood. God took this commandment very seriously. Later in the nation's history, the Lord accused the people of robbing Him through the prophet Malachi. In one passage, the Israelites ask Him, "In what way have we robbed You?"[10] In response to their question, God says:

> "In tithes and offerings. You are cursed with a curse, for you have robbed Me, even this whole nation. Bring all the tithes into the storehouse, that there may be food in My house, and try Me now in this," says the Lord of hosts, "If I will not open for you the windows of heaven and pour out for you such blessing that there will not be room enough to receive it." (**Malachi 3:8-10**)

In this dialogue, we see that the Lord did not consider tithing to be optional. In fact, He viewed withholding the tithe as theft. And He challenged His people to test Him through the practice of tithing. He promised an abundance of blessings to His people if they obeyed Him in this command. The tithe accomplished three things: it was a test of the people's trust in God, a way to provide for the Levitical priesthood and an opportunity for God's people to experience abundant blessings for their obedience.

## TITHING AND THE NEW TESTAMENT

What about the concept of tithing in the New Testament? Are believers today required to obey the same Old Covenant commandments? These are legitimate questions that Christians should ask. References to the practice of tithing in the New Testament are few. Jesus mentions this principle when he rebuked the Pharisees in Matthew 23:23. He highlights the fact that, although these religious leaders were meticulous to tithe everything they had, they were neglecting more important heart issues.

Another example occurs when Jesus gives the parable of the tax collector and the Pharisee in Luke 18. In this story, the Pharisee calls attention to his faithfulness in tithing as supposed evidence of his spirituality. Jesus again makes the point that practicing the outward principle means nothing if our hearts are not pure before God. In neither case does He suggest that tithing should no longer be practiced, but that it must be done with proper motives.

Other than another obscure reference in Hebrews relating to Abraham's tithe to Melchizedek,[11] the New Testament is silent on the issue. Financial giving is spoken of on multiple occasions, but not the specific practice of tithing. Because of this, a Christian's responsibility when it comes to tithing is a topic that is widely debated. On one side, there are those who believe that the tithe is a biblical command that still applies today and that every Christian must pay it or come under a curse, as described in the Old Testament. On the other side, there are those who see the tithe as part of the Old Covenant Law, and therefore, no longer required of us. Personally, I think it is important for us to not consider tithing solely in the context of the Mosaic Law, but instead, to examine its value and importance based on its intended purpose.

As stated in the previous section, the tithe accomplished three primary things:

1. The tithe was a test of the people's trust in God.
2. The tithe was a way to provide for the priesthood.
3. The tithe was an opportunity for God's people to experience the blessings of obedience.

All three of these purposes are still valid when it comes to the practice of tithing for New Testament Christians. Tithing is still a very effective way to test our trust in the Lord. The tithe is also used to provide for the local church, including its staff and programs, similar to the Levitical priesthood of the Old Testament. And it is certainly still an opportunity to experience incredible blessings from God. When someone begins to question the validity of the practice for New Testament believers, my question is, "Whether or not the Lord requires it anymore, why would I not want to freely give the Lord a portion of my finances on a regular basis? And why not start with a tenth since there is a biblical precedent for it? What is the downside of freely giving the Lord a percentage of my income to further His Kingdom and open the doors of heaven over my finances?"

Tithing is an extremely practical way to become good stewards of God's resources, even as modern-day believers. It is intended to be a regular reminder that everything we have belongs to Him. As stewards, we should realize that the Lord could ask for one hundred percent of our money and be completely justified. Asking for ten percent of our income is not only His right, but a very small sacrifice on our part compared to all that He has blessed us with. Tithing helps us learn to hold loosely to our finances and condition ourselves to act as stewards—rather than owners—of our money.

## SACRIFICIAL OFFERINGS

The tithe is given from the first ten percent of our income. It is a principle that we practice as an act of obedience to God. But faithful tithing is only the first step into this life of financial surrender. Anything above our tithe is an offering and an act of sacrifice to Him. While we do not need to pray for guidance about how much to tithe (because the Word of God gives us a specific percentage), we should include the leading of the Lord when it comes to sacrificial giving in excess of our tithe.

Under the Old Covenant, sacrificial offerings were acts of giving that took place on a regular basis. Each type of offering had its own unique purpose, but all were presented to the Lord from the people's resources. These offerings were a tangible expression of sacrificial worship to God. Some of the sacrifices were commanded by the Lord, such as burnt sacrifices for atonement.[12] Others, called freewill offerings, were given voluntarily by the people as they determined.[13] Sacrificial offerings were given above and beyond the tithing requirement. It was another regular reminder to God's people that their resources were not theirs alone.

Under the New Covenant, the sacrificial system is no longer required. But we should still desire to take part in voluntary, sacrificial giving to the Lord. Though our giving looks much different than it did in the Old Testament, the purpose of it remains the same. We do not bring animals and crops to a temple, but we do give funds physically and digitally to churches and other ministries. When we give out of our abundance, it is a tangible expression of worship to the God who faithfully provides all for us. While the Israelites were told when and where to give their sacrifices and offerings, as New Testament believers, we are able to cooperate with the Holy Spirit to determine how our money can be invested into the Kingdom of God.

The opportunities to sow financial seed into God's work on the earth are vast. Here are a few common ways that believers sacrificially give:

- Toward ministries and programs provided by our local church

- Toward national and international missionaries
- Toward organizations that share the Gospel in specific ways:
  - Anti-Human Trafficking Ministries
  - Women's Pregnancy Centers
  - Evangelistic Ministries
  - Drug and Alcohol Programs
  - Homeless Ministries
- Toward specific families or projects as needs are brought to our attention

When we keep our eyes open for ways to invest in people and ministries with our finances, we will find opportunities all around us. We can develop the skill of becoming sensitive to the prompting of the Holy Spirit as to where and how much we should give. Sacrificial giving turns our finances into a powerful weapon to see the Kingdom of God expand on the earth, rather than a way for us to spend selfishly on ourselves.

Numbers 15:3 tells us that the offerings that the people brought to the Lord were a sweet-smelling aroma to Him. Though we no longer burn animal sacrifices, the same aroma goes before the Lord from those who willingly give of their resources. Offerings are a voluntary expression of worship to the God who gave everything for us. As we give to the Lord above and beyond our tithes, we open the door for increased blessing in our lives through our generosity.

## THE LINK BETWEEN FINANCES AND FAITH

Despite the clear teaching of Scripture and God's promises regarding financial stewardship, this area can be a real obstacle for Christians. When our perspective about giving is faulty, it can make obedience in this area seem like an insurmountable task. Some have allowed misconceptions about giving to prevent them from stepping out in faith in their finances. They might reason with themselves, "I can't afford to give to the Lord. I am struggling financially as it is!" The truth is that we cannot afford *not* to give. The blessings that come from being faithful in this area far outweigh the sacrifice it takes.

Others incorrectly view tithes and offerings as money that could be better spent on other things. In their perspective, to give money away—even to further the cause of God's Kingdom—requires that they choose between generosity and taking care of their own needs and desires. Again, because the Lord rewards us for our generosity, this "either-or" perspective does not take into consideration the element of faith. Personally, I have never met a believer who has truly surrendered their finances to the Lord who thinks that way. I have not heard anyone say, "I wish I could go back over the years and get my tithes and offerings back so that I could spend that money on other things." Instead, I have heard countless testimonies about how God has proven Himself faithful to those who allow their faith to impact their finances.

Regardless of the reasoning a believer may give for their lack of financial surrender, there is often a deeper underlying issue, and that is a lack of trust. Some are just looking for excuses because they do not really trust the Lord to be faithful. And because they refuse to test Him in this area, they never experience the blessing that comes from stewarding God's resources well. He is calling them to step out on the water, but they are waiting for the assurance that they will not sink before they take the first step. But that is not how faith operates. We must give faithfully in obedience and sacrifice. When we do our part, the Lord will do His by pouring His blessings into our lives in the way that He chooses. The following principles should encourage all of us to take a step of faith and learn to surrender our finances in a fuller way.

## PRINCIPLES OF NEW TESTAMENT GIVING

Paul provides us with guidelines on financial giving in his letter to the church in Corinth. At the time of his writing, the Corinthian believers were preparing to give an offering to another group of Christians in need. We will highlight several verses to glean New Testament principles on how we should give to the Lord and His Kingdom.

**Principle #1: You Reap What You Sow**

*He who sows sparingly will also reap sparingly, and he who sows bountifully will also reap bountifully. **(2 Corinthians 9:6)***

In verse 6, Paul references the principle of reaping and sowing as it relates to giving. What we receive is always in proportion to our generosity. That being said, we should never be motivated by a selfish desire to receive something from the Lord. Some ministers are guilty of extorting this principle by making promises like, "If you give one-hundred dollars to our ministry, God will give you a thousand back." This type of teaching breeds a covetous heart and is contrary to the way the Lord wants us to give. Giving to the Lord is a relational practice, not a mathematical formula. If we are generous in our giving, the Lord will bless us with His generosity.

**Principle #2: Giving Should Not Be Burdensome**

*So let each one give as he purposes in his heart, not grudgingly or of necessity; for God loves a cheerful giver. **(2 Corinthians 9:7)***

Financial surrender should never be a burden. It should not feel like a lifeless transaction, as if we are paying a utility bill. Neither should we give from of a sense of guilt or merely out of obligation. Instead, our hearts should be filled with the joy of sowing our resources into God's Kingdom. The Greek word for *cheerful* describes someone who is ready to give because they are already persuaded or inclined to do so.[14] They are not wrestling internally with the decision, but full of joy about it. The way to become a cheerful giver is to fully embrace the Lord's promises to us in this area. When we know that He is pleased with the way we are handling our finances, we can invest our money in His Kingdom with excitement and expectation.

### Principle #3: You Cannot Out-Give God

*And God is able to make all grace abound toward you, that you, always having all sufficiency in all things, may have an abundance for every good work.* **(2 Corinthians 9:8)**

Paul goes on to explain that the Lord will meet all our needs, all the time. This is why we should never resist becoming generous givers. When giving sacrificially, we should not be concerned about giving "too much." The saying is true that you cannot out-give God. When given the opportunity, make it a practice to ask the Holy Spirit to speak to you about the right amount to give. Be willing to allow Him to stretch you out of your comfort zone in this area. It can be frightening when we give more than we can comfortably afford. But it is also exhilarating to truly walk in faith, believing God's Word that He will provide everything that we need as we are led by His Spirit.

### Principle #4: We Are Blessed to Be a Blessing

*You will be made rich in every way so that you can be generous in every way.* **(2 Corinthians 9:11 CEB)**

This Scripture shows us the reason for the blessings God gives to us. We are blessed to have an abundance so that we can bless others! Spiritual riches come to us in many ways. The Bible promises us that as we give, God will make us rich *in every way* so that we can then pour out those blessings into the lives of other people. The more that we give, the more that we receive, which makes us able to give even more!

The privilege we have as believers to cooperate with the Lord's work through our finances is nothing short of amazing. You and I have the ability to team up with God and provide resources to see His Kingdom expand in the lives of other people on this earth. He does not need our money to accomplish His goals, but He set up a system that allows us to partner with Him and be blessed for it. With these principles in mind, what could stop us from desiring to grow in the area of financial stewardship?

# THE BLESSING OF FINANCIAL SURRENDER

Over the years, I have spoken with many believers about finances in various settings. You can always identify the ones who have been practicing financial stewardship, because their eyes light up at the topic. They cannot wait to share all the remarkable stories of how the Lord has proven His faithfulness to them throughout the years. I am astounded at the creative ways that God finds to bless His children financially. This is not to say that the Lord will never provide for the needs of a Christian who withholds generosity to some extent. But because of the principles of Scripture and His faithfulness to honor His Word, there is a special blessing to those who test Him in this area.

My story is no exception. When I first got saved, I was taught the concept of tithing as a basic principle of discipleship. I never questioned it or tried to justify not practicing it. I saw it clearly taught in the Bible, believed it and put it into practice. In my childlike faith, trying to find a way to absolve myself of the responsibility to tithe never occurred to me. So, I started practicing it and I never looked back. I just assumed that it was standard practice for the Christian life, and it seemed a small sacrifice for all the Lord had done for me.

My wife also faithfully tithed throughout her life, having been saved at a young age. When we were married, we never withheld our tithe, even when our finances were tight. We also gave sacrificially to missions and other Christian ministries. We have challenged ourselves to intentionally grow in generosity. And our testimony is that the Lord always provided for us financially in countless ways.

Over the years, I have seen the Lord supernaturally provide for our family as we have trusted Him in this area. We have seen miraculous provision and have made it through seasons that could have been financially devastating if the Lord had not intervened. Sometimes, we see legitimate financial miracles, such as a check in the mail at the exact time it is needed, or debt being eliminated from unexpected sources. But most of the time, it looks like an endless series of small financial breakthroughs that carry us throughout life.

When we look at our budget, there have been seasons when it is impossible to understand how the Lord stretches our finances. I have often wondered if He makes our gasoline go further or our food last longer than other people. I have even speculated if it is possible that we have experienced money supernaturally multiplying in our bank accounts. But knowing precisely how the Lord's blessing operates in our lives is unimportant. All we need to know is that God has been, and will continue to be, faithful to us. And we believe His blessing is a direct result of our faithfulness to Him.

Because of this, I am personally grateful for the biblical principles of tithing and sacrificial giving. I do not see it as some mandatory requirement that I need to obey or pay the penalty. I see it as an opportunity to show the Lord how much I trust Him, help expand the Kingdom of God through our local church and around the world and provide an open door for the blessing of God in our lives. While some in the church may roll their eyes when it comes time to take up the offering, we have truly become joyful givers, because it has been such a tangible demonstration of the faithfulness of God in our lives.

As this chapter comes to a close, take a moment to ask yourself the following questions to apply these principles in a practical way:

- Am I faithfully tithing 10% of my income?
- If not, what is the reason I am withholding it?
- Do I truly trust the Lord to take care of my needs as I steward His resources well?
- What is one way that I can step out further in faith in my finances?
- How can I further develop a generous heart toward the Lord?

Take some time to examine your life in this area and be willing to take it to the Lord in prayer. Dig into the Scriptures and find out what God has to say about financial stewardship. And be willing to step out in deeper surrender in this important area of the Crucified Lifestyle.

# SECTION FOUR:

## A DISCIPLINED LIFESTYLE

Picture yourself standing in front of a descending escalator. An extravagant gift is waiting for you at the top, representing the abundant life that Jesus promises His followers. The escalator is illustrative of the uphill battle that we often face due to the devil, sin, the world and our flesh.

Too many have grown comfortable standing at the bottom of the escalator with the thought, "That gift that God is offering sounds amazing, but I don't think I can climb these steps to get it." We look around at other Christians who are also standing with us at the bottom, and their presence reinforces our decision to remain where we stand. Some have made an attempt, but have since given up because the resistance was too great, returning to the bottom in defeat. We wonder if there is any use even trying.

But there are some—many of whom are reading these words—who will see the prize and be willing to fight for it. They are tired of sitting on the sidelines and want to enter more fully into the abundant life that Jesus offers. They refuse to believe that the status quo Christian experience common in the church today is God's best for them. Regardless of what other professing Christians do, they are going to begin to take the necessary steps to obtain everything that Jesus' death and resurrection has made available. And the Lord has given us practical tools to help us get there.

We have now examined the Crucified Lifestyle through three distinct lenses: definition, victory and surrender. In this fourth and final section of the book, we will be analyzing the cross-centered life through the lens of discipline. In the following three chapters, we will discuss three spiritual disciplines: self-denial, maturity and intimacy. Each has a unique role in helping us live the lifestyle of Crucified Christians.

"Once he loses his heart for 'self' the believer can be wholly God's."

-Watchman Nee[1]

CHAPTER

9

## THE DISCIPLINE OF SELF-DENIAL

*Crucified Christians Practice Saying "No" to Themselves*

OUR SINFUL FLESH HATES DISCIPLINE because it will always resist anything that aims to weaken its control. Learning to live under the guidance and influence of the Holy Spirit requires that we keep our flesh from becoming the dominating force in our lives. In Galatians 5:24, Paul makes this assertion: "Those who are Christ's have crucified the flesh with its passions and desires." Scripture teaches us that the Crucified Lifestyle and self-denial are a package deal.

Jesus also made the same connection in Luke 9 when He said that all His disciples must deny themselves. That Greek word for *deny* is *arneomai*, and simply means to say "No."[2] We could insert that definition into Luke 9:23 and it would read, "If anyone desires to come after Me, let him *continually tell himself no*, and take up his cross daily, and follow Me." In our journey of faith, we are required to die to our flesh on a regular basis. It is not a matter of *if* but *when*. And that *when* occurs every day—one decision at a time—as we choose to live for God's desires rather than our own.

Neither Paul nor Jesus was trying to express an obscure theological concept when they spoke about the denial of self. Rather, they were describing a principle with very practical application to our lives. To talk about self-denial sounds spiritual and even somewhat mystical. But in this chapter, we will discuss a very tangible expression of self-denial, and that is fasting.

## THE ROLE OF SELF IN THE CHRISTIAN LIFE

To understand the crucial role that self-denial plays in the Crucified Lifestyle, it is necessary to explain the biblical concept of *self* in more depth. When we use the term self in relation to the life of a believer, we are not talking about the person that God designed us to be as His children. In His wisdom and creativity, God hand-crafted each of us with unique personalities, talents, desires and physical attributes. The Bible says that we are "fearfully and wonderfully made."[3] Each of us has the capacity to glorify God through our lives in a distinct way. In that sense, who we are is very precious to the Lord.

However, there is a part of our being that remains tied to the sinful state into which we were born. This is the fallen nature that all humans (with the exception of Jesus) share as descendants of Adam. Various translations of the Bible refer to it as "the flesh," "the sinful nature" or the "carnal mind." Paul speaks about this in Romans 8:7-8:

- Because the *carnal mind* is enmity against God; for it is not subject to the law of God, nor indeed can be. (**NKJV**)

- The *mind governed by the flesh* is hostile to God; it does not submit to God's law, nor can it do so. (**NIV**)

- For the *sinful nature* is always hostile to God. It never did obey God's laws, and it never will. (**NLT**)

The Greek word used in this verse is *sarks*. In the New Testament, this term is most often used with a negative connotation, and is defined in the following way:

> In short, flesh generally relates to unaided human effort, i.e. decisions that originate from self or are empowered by self. This is carnal and proceeds out of the untouched part of us – i.e. what is not transformed by God.[4]

Robert South expounds further:

> By flesh we are to understand the whole entire body of sin and corruption, that inbred proneness in our nature to all evil…that fuel or combustible matter in the soul, that is apt to be fired by every temptation; the womb that conceives and brings forth all actual impurities.[5]

Essentially, the flesh refers to the part of us that remains unredeemed on the earth and in rebellion against God. Our sinful nature is self-centered and self-protective, and it attempts to use our mind, will and emotions to pursue things that are outside of God's will for us.

When we come to Christ, our old sinful nature is crucified with Him, and we receive a new nature in its place. Although that crucifixion becomes a spiritual reality when we are born again, it also requires an ongoing process of learning to die to our flesh and live according to our new identity in Christ. Some scholars describe this dichotomy as two types of sanctification that occur in every believer's life. The first is positional sanctification, which occurs at the moment of conversion. The second is progressive sanctification, which happens as we mature in the faith and become increasingly conformed to the image of Jesus.[6] All believers live in this spiritual tension that comes from our sinful nature being both crucified and requiring continual crucifixion. Though our flesh has been dealt a death blow at the cross, we still have the choice to live according to our old nature rather than our new nature in Christ. If we had no desire to live for ourselves, there would be nothing preventing us from entering into the Crucified Lifestyle with reckless abandon.

## OUR OWN WORST ENEMIES

When we make Jesus the Lord of our lives, essentially, we are communicating to Him, "Here is my life. Teach me how to follow you as your disciple." Our new Master is supposed to start calling the shots and we are simply to follow and obey Him to the best of our ability. However, anyone who has walked with Christ knows that it is not that easy. This is because our sinful nature fights with the Holy Spirit for dominance over our lives. The greatest challenge that most of us face will not come from external forces, but from the internal force that refuses to submit to the Lord's authority. When we came to faith, we entered into a spiritual combat zone that is unique to believers. Gottfried Osei-Mensah summarizes this battle we all face:

> The Christian lives in a fallen world with all its tensions. Nevertheless, we are new creatures filled with the power of the Holy Spirit and with the longings for holiness which he puts within us. A heavenly value system now characterizes our lives here in this fallen world. Anyone who lives in such a context is bound to live in tremendous tension and be pulled in different directions… As long as we are on this earth there is a civil war going on.[7]

This battle between our natures can only be won with the Lord's help. The flesh cannot be redeemed or negotiated with. We will never convince it to obey God or to change its ways. The only way to overcome its power is to crucify it.

In the natural realm, we experience this tension every time we are faced with temptation. When presented with an opportunity to please our sinful flesh through our imagination or some external stimulus, our spiritual man wants to resist the temptation and obey the Lord. But there is a part of us that desires the pleasures of sin. Our sinful nature would rather give into temptation due to whatever perceived benefit it promises us. In those moments, we make the choice which nature we allow to have its way. Every temptation is a test to see if we will submit to the Lord and His rule over our lives, or rebel against Him and please our flesh. In those moments, we need to be trained to say "No" to temptation. And this is something we must continually practice throughout our time on this earth.

## CRUCIFYING THE OLD MAN

Ofer Amitai says, "We don't need to try harder, but we need to die better."[8] My own experience testifies to this truth because I can trace just about every problem that I have faced in my discipleship journey to a lack of flesh-crucifixion. Often, when I bemoan my struggles to the Lord, I hear Him gently say, "Son, the reason you are struggling is because you are refusing to die to your flesh." The reality is that most of my battles come from an unwillingness to control, deny and die to self. While I often try to blame other people or situations, when I really get honest with myself, I realize that my selfish motives and responses are far greater contributors than any other factor.

In Galatians 2:20, Paul makes the bold statement, "I have been crucified with Christ; it is no longer I who live, but Christ lives in me." Paul understood that his old self had been united with Jesus in His crucifixion. He used the past tense to describe this death that had already taken place. This thought is echoed in several of his letters:

- …knowing this, that our old man was crucified with Him, that the body of sin might be done away with, that we should no longer be slaves of sin. (**Romans 6:6**)

- Therefore, if anyone is in Christ, he is a new creation; old things have passed away; behold, all things have become new. (**2 Corinthians 5:17**)

- ...that you put off, concerning your former conduct, the old man which grows corrupt according to the deceitful lusts... **(Ephesians 4:22)**

- Do not lie to one another, since you have put off the old man with his deeds... **(Colossians 3:9)**

Paul uses the illustration of two opposing persons in his description of our spiritual lives. The first is our old man that has been crucified with Christ when we repented and were saved. The second is our new man that has been united with Christ in His resurrection. Paul uses this language to help us understand the battle that we all face between our natures. The Apostle is basically saying, "We used to be completely different people. We were sinners and rebels against God. But now we are entirely new people in Christ."

In the Colossians verse above, Paul explains that we have a responsibility to "put off" the old man. The Greek word he uses means to, "completely strip off, thoroughly renounce."[9] This is another way of illustrating what it means to put our flesh to death. The problem that we face is that the old man does not stay in the grave. It tends to rise up when we crave something for selfish pleasure. Through temptation, that sinful nature that we thought was dead will rise again and attempt to thwart our desire to obey the Lord. However, the thought of entertaining anything that our flesh wants should disturb us. As Robert Mounce suggests,

> The very idea of responding positively to sin's invitation should strike the believer as morbid. For the Christian to choose to sin is the spiritual equivalent of digging up a corpse for fellowship.[10]

As horrific of a mental image as that gives us, it is an accurate depiction of what takes place spiritually when we give into our flesh as believers. How could we attempt to live with something that God has declared dead? Grasping the spiritual reality of being crucified with Christ should dramatically change the way we do life.

# SELF-CONTROL OVER SELF-INDULGENCE

The Scriptures elevate self-control as a desirable and necessary character quality for God's people. Here are a few of the numerous passages:

- Paul tells us that self-control is a part of the fruit that comes from living in the Spirit. **(Galatians 5:22-23)**

- Peter tells us that if we want to be fruitful, one of the things we need to practice is self-control. **(2 Peter 1:5-8)**

- When Paul is sharing the Gospel with Felix, the Scriptures say that he specifically talked to him about self-control. **(Acts 24:25)**

- We are told that someone who cannot control himself is like a city without walls. **(Proverbs 25:28)**

- James says that practicing self-control in our words helps us to steer our whole body. **(James 3:2)**

- Paul tells us that God has given us a spirit of self-control. **(2 Timothy 1:7 NIV)**

- We are told that those who rule their own spirit are better than those who can conquer a city. **(Proverbs 16:32)**

- Paul says that he disciplines his body to keep it under control. **(1 Corinthians 9:27)**

These Scriptures reveal to us that God has placed a high value on the discipline of self-control. He expects His people to practice it as a lifestyle. Those who cannot control themselves are painted in a negative light. When the Bible speaks about self, it is clear that we are not to freely indulge it or cater to it, but rather learn to keep it in check. The more that we practice these Scriptural truths, the more self-controlled we become.

While it might seem that living self-controlled lives would be overly restrictive, the opposite is true. The more our sinful flesh is dethroned in our lives, the more freedom we will enjoy. The opposite of self-control is self-indulgence, which is a life of slavery to our passions and desires. Paul tells us that, "he who sows to his flesh will of the flesh reap corruption, but he who sows to the Spirit will of the Spirit reap everlasting life."[11] The fruit of our lives is determined by the seeds that we sow. Self-control has spiritual blessings attached to it, while self-indulgence brings harmful consequences.

The greatest model that we have of a self-controlled life comes from Jesus Himself. He said "No" to many temptations in His life, including the desire for romance or elevation to fame and fortune. While He could have become a powerful ruler or a popular celebrity, He chose to deny Himself those opportunities to live for the glory of His Father. As His disciples, we should also have a willingness to deny ourselves anything that the Lord asks of us.

## THE FORGOTTEN DISCIPLINE

Now that we have established a deeper understanding of the concept of self in the Christian life, let us examine the spiritual discipline that has the power to help us overcome this battle with our flesh. Biblical fasting is the discipline of going without food for a designated time in order to seek the Lord. Fasting was once seen as a regular part of the corporate and individual lives of God's people in both Old and New Testament times. Despite the numerous references to fasting in Scripture, as well as the emphasis that the early church placed on it, the discipline of fasting is often neglected in many modern Western churches.

Jesus' command to deny ourselves in Luke 9:23 is utterly counter-cultural. As we have already discussed, the world's message is, "Promote self, Please self and Protect self." This self-centered lifestyle is elevated and advertised all around us. Because of this, selfish living requires no practice or effort. All we need to do is go along with the dominant culture around us, and we will build our lives around ourselves. This makes fasting an especially unattractive discipline in our culture. However, due to the intense pressure to live egocentric lives in the world, the value of learning how to deny ourselves is perhaps of greater urgency than ever before.

The primary reason for fasting—as is true of all the spiritual disciplines—is to foster intimacy in our relationship with the Lord. But there are secondary benefits that are also incredibly valuable. Fasting involves a very tangible form of self-denial and is one of the most practical ways that we can learn how to say "No" to ourselves. This aspect of fasting is the reason it is so intricately connected with the Crucified Lifestyle.

## WHO WILL DOMINATE OUR LIVES?

Humans eat not only for enjoyment, but also because of the nutrients that food provides. God created our hunger drive with certain stimuli, such as taste buds and our sense of smell, to drive us to eat in order to sustain life. But any physical drive that produces pleasure carries with it the danger of overindulgence or abuse. If eating was not a pleasurable experience, fasting would not be something we resist near as much as we do. However, due to the fact that our bodies have a hunger drive that causes us to intensely crave food, we experience both mental and physical resistance to any attempt of abstinence from food.

In the West, we are continually surrounded with opportunities to indulge our flesh. Grocery store shelves are stocked with every food group you can imagine. Restaurants offer cuisine from around the world. An extensive range of quality is available to us, from fast food to exquisite gourmet. Most of us have access to delivery services that will bring food from our favorite restaurants right to our front door. Many of our holidays and social gatherings are centered around food. Opportunities to eat are impossible to isolate ourselves from, which makes fasting that much more challenging. And our flesh has no desire to resist the constant temptation to indulge itself. This is why fasting is such an effective way to give our spiritual man a chance to exercise its authority over our sinful nature.

Every moment of fasting is a continual reminder from our flesh that we want to eat. I was on an extended fast recently, and someone asked me if it gets easier the longer you fast. My response was, "From the first day, I haven't gone one second without realizing I was fasting." Your body is not going to let you forget that you are keeping it from the nutrition that it needs. And so, the fast becomes a continual message to our flesh that our spiritual man is in control and we will not be dominated by selfish desires.

When I go through a stretch of time that I do not fast on a regular basis, I can feel my fleshly nature strengthening. My spiritual sensitivity grows dull and my thought life becomes less disciplined. I notice that my words are less guarded and my actions more selfish. Not too long ago, I went through a period of several weeks without a fast. When I finally set time aside for it, it was as if my spirit man was rising up inside of me, towering over the flesh, pointing his finger at the old man, saying, "You stand down! You are not going to call the shots around here." Fasting is like taking the reins of a horse that is going its own way, pulling back and saying, "Whoa! I am the driver here, not you." This is why setting aside regular time to fast is so valuable in this fight against our old nature.

Fasting teaches us to walk in the Spirit. During a fast, when our flesh cries out to be fed, we are not only saying "No" to ourselves, but "Yes" to the Lord. There is a spiritual transaction that occurs. Fasting is an expression of our love and devotion to God. We are saying, "I'm willing to go without sustenance so that I can have more of you." It causes our spirit man to thrive and our fleshly man to starve.

## DEAD MAN IN TRAINING

Another way to view fasting is as a spiritual training ground. Consider the baseball player who wants to become a professional pitcher. How many thousands of times will he pitch the ball in practice, long before pitching his first professional game? The reason that he spends so much time in preparation is so that the discipline will become automatic through training. He wants to develop muscle memory, which allows him to repeat a practiced action without conscious thought. When the time comes to play the real game, how well he has practiced will make all the difference as to how he will perform.

Training can also help prepare us for real life scenarios. I remember when the local police department came to our middle school for a "Just Say No" campaign. The idea was to introduce us to the concept of illegal

# NINE: THE DISCIPLINE OF SELF-DENIAL

drugs in an effort to train our minds to resist temptation before we came into contact with them in real life. When we would eventually encounter drugs, the program was designed to make it easier to resist because we had already been programmed to say "No" to them in the training.

Preparation is the primary purpose of all training. Whether that is to learn what it feels like to pitch a baseball correctly or to prepare to refuse peer pressure, the end goal is to have learned a skill by experience before you actually perform it. This is similar to denying ourselves through fasting. For many Christians, eating food is not the real battle. Unless they are struggling with overindulgence, the food itself is not the actual substance that they need to learn to fight. However, when we deny ourselves food, it trains us to live with self-control in other areas as well. When temptations come in other forms, our flesh has already been weakened, and we are able to respond with the spiritual strength and grace that comes from a fasted lifestyle.

Paul talks about the spiritual training of self-denial in his letter to Titus:

> For the grace of God has appeared, bringing salvation for all people, training us to renounce ungodliness and worldly passions, and to live self-controlled, upright, and godly lives in the present age… **(Titus 2:11-12 ESV)**

Here, we see a picture of grace personified as a personal trainer. One of the practical functions of God's grace is to train believers to resist ungodly passions and to control self. We have been given God's empowering grace to help us in this spiritual training ground. Those who take the time to learn to deny themselves through fasting will have a huge advantage when ungodliness and worldly passions are presented to them.

## OUR FLESH HATES BEING DENIED

Fasting can be a very challenging discipline. Even as I write these words, I am planning to begin an extended fast tomorrow. I can already feel my flesh whining, like a spoiled child throwing a temper tantrum, tempting me to reconsider. The old man is shouting, "Don't go on a fast. Why would you want to do that? You are going to be so miserable. Just put it off a little longer. There will be a better time."

The reality is that if I wait until I feel like fasting, I will never do it. My flesh absolutely despises it. I often get a pit in my stomach a couple of days before a fast just planning for it. Because of this, there are always excuses for cancelling a fast before it begins. It seems that there is always a special dinner, party or social gathering right when I plan to fast. It is so easy to put it off until a more convenient day, which never comes. This is why waiting to fast until we feel specifically led by the Lord can actually prevent us from doing it at all. Because of this, fasting requires diligence, determination and intentionality on our part, along with the grace of God and the help of the Holy Spirit.

Those who endeavor to live the Crucified Lifestyle will discover that crucifying the flesh is a daily task and one that does not happen without a battle. As Robert South stated about dying to the flesh:

> This is a greater work than men are aware of. It is indeed the killing of an enemy, but of such an enemy as a man thinks his friend, and loves as his child; and how hard it is to put the knife to the throat of an Isaac is easily imaginable. What! Part with that that came into the world with me, and has ever since lived and conversed with me, that continually lies down and rises up with me, that has even incorporated itself into my nature, seized all my appetites, and possessed all my faculties, so that it is the centre and principle of all my pleasures, and that which gives a relish and a quickness to every object! This is a hard saying, and a harder undertaking.[12]

Yet, despite the battle, the benefits of denying ourselves are incredible. As we learn to die to self, our new nature in Christ becomes more dominate in our lives. We find ourselves increasingly filled with the character qualities of the Holy Spirit. We become a blessing to those around us and walk in a peace and joy that simply cannot be attained any other way. The intimacy that we can experience with the Lord is worth any momentary struggle that we may face. So let the flesh cry out and complain! It will always resist the things of God and will keep us from living the Crucified Lifestyle if we bow down to its requests.

## THE AROMA OF SACRIFICE

I was reading in the Book of Leviticus recently and found multiple passages that described sacrifices as "a sweet aroma to the Lord."[13] The thought occurred to me that God loves the smell of burnt offerings. Those sacrifices that the people burned on the altar released a scent into the atmosphere. But it was not the actual aroma of burning animals that the Lord enjoyed. Rather, it was the fragrance that came from His people's desire to obey His commands and have fellowship with Him.

Paul tells us in Romans 12:1 that we should present our "bodies a living sacrifice, holy, acceptable to God." You and I have opportunities every day to bring a sacrifice to the Lord. We choose whether or not our lives are a sweet-smelling aroma to Him. Fasting is one of the ways that we can apply this verse practically. There are moments during a fast when you feel too weak to pray or study the Word of God. You simply do not have the energy to do anything but rest. In those moments, I like to think of myself as a sacrifice laid down on the altar for the Lord. I realize that even in those moments when my strength is sapped, there is still an aroma rising from my life to Heaven. It is the smell of sacrifice; the scent of my old nature being put to death. And God loves the aroma that comes from His people practicing self-denial to seek after Him.

Let us each take the time to consider how much the discipline of fasting is having an impact on our spiritual lives. Are we actively engaging with this powerful practice or have we set it aside due to a lack of desire or knowledge about its potential impact?

I will close this chapter with a convicting thought from C.S. Lewis:

> Christ says 'Give me All. I don't want so much of your time and so much of your money and so much of your work: I want You. I have not come to torment your natural self, but to kill it. No half measures are any good. I don't want to cut off a branch here and a

branch there, I want to have the whole tree down. I don't want to drill the tooth, or crown it, or stop it, but to have it out. Hand over the whole natural self, all the desires which you think innocent as well as the ones you think wicked—the whole outfit. I will give you a new self instead. In fact, I will give you Myself: My own will shall become yours.'[14]

My prayer for each of us is that we will be willing to say "Yes" to the Lord in this beautiful, but sometimes painful journey of self-denial called the Crucified Lifestyle. In the next chapter, we will learn about the crucial discipline of maturity.

"Sanctification means being made one with Jesus so that the disposition that ruled Him will rule us...It will cost everything that is not of God in us."

-Oswald Chambers[1]

CHAPTER

10

## THE DISCIPLINE OF MATURITY

*Crucified Christians Grow Spiritually
Through Scripture Interaction*

LONG BEFORE JESUS WALKED THE earth and announced His call to discipleship in Luke 9, God was already calling people into a relationship with Himself. The storyline of God's relational invitation to mankind is recorded in a collection of writings that we now refer to as the Bible. Without the Word of God, we would left alone to navigate our faith journey. But because of the Scriptures, we have been provided with everything we need to understand how to live in rich communion with our Creator.

Due to its revelatory teaching about how to know and serve the Living God, the Bible is the most important book in existence. While some claim that it is only a collection of moral instruction, religious tradition or cultural history, none of these descriptions fully encapsulate the qualities that make the Judeo-Christian Scriptures unique from every other book ever written. The Scriptures testify about themselves in a way that no other literature does. 2 Timothy 3:16 tells us that, "All Scripture is given by inspiration of God." Hebrews 4:12 states, "For the word of God is living and powerful." The significance and relevance of the Bible come from its source. Although God used humans to record the words, the Scriptures testify that the Holy Spirit provided the inspiration. As Peter wrote,

> ...knowing this first, that no prophecy of Scripture is of any private interpretation, for prophecy never came by the will of man, but holy men of God spoke as they were moved by the Holy Spirit.
> **(2 Peter 1:20-21)**

Humans have produced innumerable writings throughout history. Many remarkable literary works have been instrumental in educating, inspiring and entertaining us throughout the ages. But no other writing can accomplish what the Bible can. A spiritual transaction takes place internally in the life of a believer when the Scriptures are approached in faith and humility. The Holy Spirit—who authored the Bible—is able to speak through His written Word in a way that can transform a human heart. The very life of God is transmitted to the one who approaches the Scriptures with a sincere desire to interact with the Lord. The end-product of that transfer of life is spiritual maturity.

# THE RABBI-DISCIPLE RELATIONSHIP

Spiritual maturity is a process that should be continually occurring in the life of every one of Jesus' followers. However, much of what we call discipleship in the church today falls short of the experience of the New Testament disciples. While classes and discipleship programs can play an important role in teaching new believers about following Christ, they provide only one aspect of what it means to be a disciple.

During Jesus' time, rabbis played a significant role in the Jewish educational system. Children in that culture had the opportunity to progress through three levels of education and spiritual instruction. Bet Sefer was for elementary-aged children, where they would learn to read and write as well as study and memorize the Torah. Most children would go through this foundational level of education. For those who did well in Bet Sefer, a secondary school was offered for students in their early teenaged years called Bet Midrash. This included a more intense study of the Torah and oral traditions. A few of those students who excelled in Bet Midrash could then approach a rabbi in hopes of becoming one of his disciples. This final level of education required a wholehearted commitment from the student desiring discipleship.[2]

The Hebrew word for a disciple is *talmid*. From a modern Western perspective, it is difficult to find an analogy that accurately describes the level of impact that the rabbi-talmid relationship made on his followers. This is because it is unique from most teacher-student relationships common in our society. In our culture, a student's primary objective is to learn a trade or gather information from a teacher. For example, college students sit in a classroom and receive instruction and insight from professors. The goal is to acquire the information and skills necessary to complete the course to earn a degree.

This is much different from the goal of the disciple in first century Jewish culture. In that context, the goal was to actually become *like* his rabbi. The disciple was not following the rabbi only to gain information but was to pay close attention to the lifestyle that he lived. The talmid was to imitate the rabbi and, in so doing, become like him in speech, action and pattern of life. As Ray Vander Laan explains:

> A talmid wants to be like the teacher, that is to become what the teacher is. That meant that students were passionately devoted to their rabbi and noted everything he did or said. This meant the rabbi-talmid relationship was a very intense and personal system of education. As the rabbi lived and taught his understanding of the Scripture his students listened and watched and imitated so as to become like him.[3]

This is the primary difference between modern discipleship methods and the discipleship of the New Testament. As followers of Christ, merely gaining information about spiritual truths is not the equivalent of biblical discipleship, which aims to conform us to the likeness of our Rabbi.

## A CALL TO FOLLOW

Jesus explained in Luke 9:23 that those who desire to become His disciples will *follow* Him. That Greek word is *akoloutheó* and has the literal meaning of joining the road with someone.[4] Our Rabbi invites us to join together with Him on His pathway. Followers of Christ are not to continue going their own way and invite Jesus to come along. Rather, discipleship involves forsaking the pathway that we once walked and choosing to walk in a different direction as we follow Jesus. No one will find themselves walking on the pathway of the Crucified Lifestyle until they make an intentional decision to abandon their own way.

Following Jesus as modern-day disciples provides a different set of challenges than what the first century disciples would have faced. After all, we do not have Jesus in human form to interact with and observe. While we do have spiritual leaders and others in the church who can teach us, it certainly feels like we are at a disadvantage without a tangible rabbi to emulate. However, the process of discipleship has not changed. It is still a call to follow our Rabbi, learn from Him and put His teachings into practice. And we are blessed to have His words, found not only in the red letters of the Bible, but throughout the rest of the Scriptures as well. The truth of God's Word, coupled with the indwelling Holy Spirit, provide all that we need to become Jesus' modern-day talmidim.

Our level of spiritual maturity is directly related to how wholeheartedly we have attempted to follow Christ. The more willing we are to die to ourselves and live for Him, the quicker we will mature. Each decision to deny ourselves and follow Christ pushes our spiritual roots deeper into the ground. The way that this transformation occurs is through simple obedience to the Word of God. Every command in the Scripture is both a call to follow Jesus and an invitation to become more like Him.

When Jesus called His early disciples, He simply said, "Follow me."[5]

## TEN: THE DISCIPLINE OF MATURITY

This is the same invitation that He gives to each one of us, every time we engage with the Word of God. Through the Scriptures, He is essentially saying, "Come, join me on my road. Learn to do things my way. Emulate me." Obedience to His commands keeps our spiritual feet on the pathway of our Rabbi.

# THE NECESSITY OF APPLICATION

The Bible has a unique interactive quality. The living Scriptures are not merely words printed on a page, but truths that demand a response from those who read them. The Word of God is meant to be applied, not simply learned, memorized or studied. Every interaction with the Scriptures has the potential to contribute to our spiritual growth. But unless the Bible is approached with a willingness and determination to put its truths into practice, there is no guarantee of life change.

This is the reason why a student can go to seminary, spend years studying the Scriptures, and dry up spiritually at the same time. One might think that the continual study of God's Word would always bring a greater measure of passion for the Lord into a person's life, but the opposite can occur if it does not become true heart-knowledge evidenced by obedience. Some will testify to the fact that the driest spiritual season in their lives happened while they were pursuing their calling through Christian education. As Edgar Elliston explains:

> We tend to believe that if we know more, we will be more…Jesus did not command, as some of us mistakenly read, to 'teach all things.' That is a serious problem many churches,' Bible colleges' and seminaries' programs now face…We strive to 'teach all things' rather than 'teach obedience in all things' He commanded. To know about is not to be. To describe is not to do. To list is not to apply. Information will not save us.[6]

We learn this lesson from the Pharisees of Jesus' time. These religious leaders had a comprehensive knowledge of God's Word. In fact, the

Pharisees spent their entire lives studying and memorizing the Old Testament Scriptures. One might assume that they would be deeply mature due to their extensive Scriptural knowledge. And yet, they were the ones who clashed with Christ and eventually had Him put to death. Jesus tried to warn them in John 5:39: "You search the Scriptures, for in them you think you have eternal life; and these are they which testify of Me. But you are not willing to come to Me that you may have life." The Pharisees' example reveals that even an intense study of the Scriptures does not guarantee spiritual maturity. It is only through sincere application that the maturation process occurs.

## THE PROCESS OF MATURITY

Spiritual maturity is the process of growth through which we become more like Christ, our Rabbi. The word *image* is a common descriptor in Paul's writings about Jesus. Paul refers to Jesus as, "the image of the invisible God"[7] and "the image of God."[8] The Greek word he uses is *eikón*, which refers to a "mirror-like representation, referring to what is very close in resemblance."[9] What is incredible is that God desires all believers to take on the same image:

> But we all, with unveiled face, beholding as in a mirror the glory of the Lord, are being transformed into the same image from glory to glory, just as by the Spirit of the Lord. **(2 Corinthians 3:18)**

The Greek word for *transformed* in this passage is *metamorphoó* and speaks of a literal change or transformation.[10] In this verse, Paul is referring to the transformational work that takes place inside of us as we behold the glory of God and become more like Him. God's desire is that every disciple is transformed into the image of Jesus. Paul repeats this thought in Romans 8:29, "For whom He foreknew, He also predestined to be conformed to the image of His Son." The word for *conformed* in this passage is *sýmmorphos*, which means to share "the same inner essence-identity."[11] Both of these terms, *transformed* and *conformed*, are descriptors of the Holy Spirit's work in making us more like the Son of God. Spiritual growth is an ongoing process through which a believer should increasingly embody the character and attributes of Christ.

The longer a person sincerely follows the Lord, the more it should become apparent that they are children of God by their character and actions. When people observed Peter and John in the book of Acts, we are told that they "were astonished and they took note that these men had been with Jesus."[12] There was a quality in the apostles' lives that reflected the time they spent with the Messiah. And it was so evident that other people could identify it by the way they lived. This process of increasing Christlikeness should take place in the lives of all of Christ's followers.

Spiritual maturity is not an automatic process, which is why someone can claim to have been saved for many years and yet remain a babe in Christ. Growth occurs as we cooperate with the maturity plan that God has designed for each of us. He uses circumstances, people, trials and a variety of other means to shape us into the image of Jesus. One cannot help but become more like Christ if we truly apply the Scriptures to our lives.

The Bible is meant to work on us like a chisel, chipping off the rough edges and unsuitable parts, so that the life of Jesus can show through. Layers of self-ambition and fleshly living need to be stripped from our hearts. Life transformation does not come from a mystical experience, but rather as our minds are renewed and become conformed to the Word of God.[13] As we hear and obey the Scriptures, we learn to die to ourselves and allow His life to be lived through us. Every command of the Bible is an invitation for us to die to our selfish desires. Whenever we come face-to-face with a principle that goes against our natural inclinations, and choose to submit to the Lord, we learn to walk increasingly in the Crucified Lifestyle. This process of maturity is often painful. But the intended result—to be fashioned into the image of Christ—is completely worth it.

# MORE THAN A BOOK OF PROMISES

Everyone loves the promises God gives us in His Word. But when we focus on the promises of the Bible at the expense of the rest of the

Scriptures, we are in dangerous territory. In fact, most of God's promises are contingent upon our willingness to walk in submission to His will and ways. When the Scriptures accomplish what God intends, they are supposed to act as a changing agent in our lives. The Bible exists, not only to encourage us, but to transform us. When Paul wrote to Timothy, he described the Scriptures this way:

> But as for you, continue in what you have learned and have become convinced of, because you know those from whom you learned it, and how from infancy you have known the Holy Scriptures, which are able to make you wise for salvation through faith in Christ Jesus. All Scripture is God-breathed and is useful for teaching, rebuking, correcting and training in righteousness, so that the servant of God may be thoroughly equipped for every good work. **(2 Timothy 3:14-17 NIV)**

In this passage, Paul reveals six significant goals for our interaction with the Scriptures.

### 1.) The Scriptures Make Us Wise for Salvation

In our natural minds, humans cannot perceive spiritual wisdom. As Paul explains in 1 Corinthians 2:14, "the natural man does not receive the things of the Spirit of God, for they are foolishness to him; nor can he know them, because they are spiritually discerned." The Lord tells us in Isaiah 55:9, "For as the heavens are higher than the earth, so are My ways higher than your ways, And My thoughts than your thoughts." While our carnal minds are not capable of grasping spiritual truth, as we interact with the Bible with the illumination of the Holy Spirit, God's wisdom is imparted to us supernaturally. This wisdom, especially as it pertains to salvation, promotes spiritual maturity in us.

## 2.) The Scriptures Teach Us

The Greek word used for *teaching* is *diaskalia*, which means, "properly applied-teaching."[14] Biblical doctrines are intended to teach us the proper way to live. Therefore, receiving Scriptural truth requires a teachable spirit. The person who approaches the Bible with a know-it-all-attitude cannot receive God's intended instruction. Our interaction with the Word of God needs to be more than an information download. Rather, it must bring practical change into our lives. This is why James warns us that we need to be doers of the Word rather than only hearers.[15] Just like Jesus' original disciples were continually indoctrinated by His Kingdom teachings, modern day disciples must become diligent students of the Bible.

## 3.) The Scriptures Rebuke Us

The Greek word, *elegchos*, means, "to convict" or "to find fault with."[16] The word *rebuke* carries a negative connotation and is most often used in the context of a confrontation with person's wrong attitude or behavior. But there is a positive aspect of being rebuked when it is done in our best interest and by someone who loves us. We all need help discovering the blind spots in our lives that stunt our spiritual growth. Interacting with the Bible is an effective way to reveal attitudes and motives that prevent us from becoming more like our Rabbi.

## 4.) The Scriptures Correct Us

*Epanorthosis*, the word translated *correcting*, refers to the process of straightening out an object, therefore making it right.[17] For example, if you hammered a nail the wrong way, causing it to bend, *epanorthosis* would describe the process of bending the nail back into its intended shape. When we live in a way that is contrary to the teachings of Scripture, our spiritual lives become bent out of shape. Much like a chiropractor can bring a spine back into alignment so that the body can function properly, the Word of God also has a way of bringing our lives into proper alignment with His will and ways through the process of correction.

### 5.) The Scriptures Train Us in Righteousness

The word for *training* in this verse is *paideia* and it refers to the process of training and educating a child.[18] In the same way that the intelligence and morality of children are developed through educational training, the Scriptures are intended to educate the believer in righteousness and the ways of God. This is why Paul tells us in Romans 12:2, "Do not be conformed to this world, but be transformed by the renewing of your mind, that you may prove what is that good and acceptable and perfect will of God." The Bible is our professor in the classroom of righteousness. As we submit ourselves to its training, we increasingly display the righteousness of Christ in our lives.

### 6.) The Scriptures Thoroughly Equip Us

Paul summarizes his instruction to Timothy by saying that we should expect to be "thoroughly equipped for every good work" as we engage with the Scriptures. This phrase comes from the Greek word *eksartizo*, which stresses the fact that the Bible "fits each believer to live in full communion with God."[19] We do not come into the Kingdom fully mature. This is why Peter encourages new believers to "desire the pure milk of the word, that you may grow thereby."[20] Each of us need to become more equipped to serve the Lord through our study and application of biblical truths.

From this passage, we can clearly see that Paul viewed the Scriptures as much more than a list of God's promises. He describes the Bible as a training manual packed with truth that should impact every aspect of our daily lives. As disciples of Christ, it is vital that we approach the Scriptures with Paul's perspective. If we are never rebuked, corrected, trained or equipped when we interact with the Bible—whether directly or through sermons or other writings—we should ask ourselves if we are truly hearing the full counsel of God. Christians who approach the Word of God only for its blessings will stay immature. The writer of Hebrews warns us about this: "For everyone who partakes only of milk is unskilled in the word of righteousness, for he is a babe."[21] God desires that we allow His Word to develop a deep maturity in our lives.

## THE SOURCE OF SPIRITUAL MATURITY

A couple of years ago, our family moved into a house with a fenced-in back yard. In the spring, I discovered a grapevine growing on the fence between us and our neighbors. While the vines looked plush and dense, the grapes only grew to a size of a couple centimeters because they had not been cultivated properly. I spoke to our neighbor and we both agreed that the grapevine was useless if it would not bear any fruit. A couple of weeks later I noticed that the vines were beginning to wilt and turn brown. A quick inspection revealed that my neighbor had severed the vine at the stem. Within days, the fruitless grapevine dried up, and I eventually removed the dead branches from the fence.

This is a picture of what Jesus was trying to convey to His followers when He shared the illustration of the vine and branches in John 15:

> I am the true vine, and My Father is the vinedresser. Every branch in Me that does not bear fruit He takes away; and every branch that bears fruit He prunes, that it may bear more fruit. You are already clean because of the word which I have spoken to you. Abide in Me, and I in you. As the branch cannot bear fruit of itself, unless it abides in the vine, neither can you, unless you abide in Me. (vss. 1-4)

As He often did in his teaching, Jesus used a natural process to reveal a spiritual principle. Even with a cursory knowledge of agriculture, the importance of the relationship between a vine and its branches is easy to appreciate. The life of a plant flows from the vine to support its branches. If a branch is separated from the vine, it is only a matter of time until that branch is dry, wilted and dead. Jesus is teaching His disciples that we need to stay intimately connected with Him in order to thrive in our Christian walk. This is why He encourages us to abide in Him. The word used for *abide* means, "to maintain unbroken fellowship with someone."[22] Just like a branch needs to maintain its connection with the grapevine in order to bear fruit, we need to remain in communion with Jesus.

Spiritual maturity is a byproduct of intimate relationship with the Lord. If we cut ourselves off from our connection with Him, we will become like that fruitless vine on our fence. We might appear to have life outwardly, but we will fail to bear any true spiritual fruit. In Jesus' illustration about the true vine and its branches, we discover two ways that God uses the Scriptures as a vehicle for spiritual transformation.

**Maturity Through Pruning**

The practice of pruning is vital to the work of a vinedresser. It is "the removal of part of a plant for the benefit of all the plant" and accomplishes three main goals: "it directs growth, it improves health and it increases production."[23] In order to promote healthy growth in a grapevine, some of its branches must be cut back. This is because all branches—even those that do not bear fruit—require energy to grow. The fruitless branches will sap a vine's energy without producing any grapes. The vinedresser must look for these energy-depleting branches and remove them to provide the plant with optimal conditions for fruit production. Anything that does not assist the vine in accomplishing its purpose must be cut off and thrown away.

Jesus uses this pruning process to describe something that God does for each of us. As already stated, God's primary purpose for His children is to form us into the image of Jesus. As the spiritual vinedresser, our Father will prune things out of our lives that work against that goal. All of us have character defects and misguided thinking that prevent us from producing spiritual fruit. We allow attitudes and wrong motives into our hearts that impede our spiritual maturity. While we may be fully convinced that we know what is best, the Lord can see the beginning from the end. He will often use a pruning process to conform us to His will and make us more like His Son.

Pruning can happen in many ways, but one of the most powerful tools the Lord uses is our interaction with the Bible. When wielded properly, the

Scriptures act like a pruning knife for our hearts. Suppose I allow a selfish attitude to take root in my life, but I do not realize it is there. As I read through the Scriptures, I come across Paul's admonition in Philippians 2:4, "Not looking to your own interests but each of you to the interests of the others." (NIV) The Holy Spirit illuminates the truth in that passage, and I become convicted about my self-centered ways. I realize as I study the passage that I have been wholly consumed with my own interests. I acknowledge my sin before the Lord, repent and ask Him for the grace to put the needs of others before my own. Later that day, I speak to a friend who is walking through a challenging situation. Rather than responding selfishly and turning the conversation toward my own needs, I offer to pray with him and listen to his problems with concern in my heart.

This is an example of how God uses His Word to prune our hearts. It takes place when we are confronted with biblical truth and we choose to repent and commit to obey the Lord in that area going forward. Approaching the Bible with an open heart enables the Holy Spirit to reveal where we need transformation in our lives. As disciples, we need to allow the Vinedresser to prune us so that He can remove branches that will stunt our spiritual growth.

**Maturity Through Purifying**

The second process that promotes spiritual maturity from John 15 is purification. In verse 3, Jesus tells His disciples, "You are already clean because of the word which I have spoken to you." The Greek word translated *clean* (*katharós*) is the adjective form of the verb *prune* in the previous verse. Although the root word is the same, most translations use the word *prune* in verse 2 and *clean* in verse 3 due to the context of the verse. The New Living Translation actually includes both words to differentiate these processes: "You have already been pruned and purified by the message I have given you."

The word *clean* in verse 3 describes a believer becoming spiritually clean by being purged or purified by God or "free from the contaminating influences of sin."[24] The word has the connotation of a deep cleansing process that purges the sin out of a person's life. Jesus' disciples do not only need to be pruned, but to undergo a purification process that removes anything from their lives that He does not want to be there.

Jesus explains to His disciples that this cleansing happened because of the word He had spoken to them. Here, He is referring to the culmination of all the teachings that He had poured into His disciples throughout His ministry. He had spent years instructing them with sermons, parables and daily life experiences. He explained many spiritual principles so that His disciples would understand how to apply what He taught. His rabbinic instruction had made a dramatic impact on each of them. They had been purified through their acceptance and obedience to His teaching.

Here are two other passages that echo this thought:

- In John 17:17, Jesus is praying for His disciples and asks His Father, "Sanctify them by your truth. Your word is truth." To be sanctified here means to "purify internally by reformation of soul."[25] In other words, Jesus is praying that God will purify the internal lives of His disciples through His word.

- In Ephesians 5:25-26, Paul speaks about Jesus' relationship to the church. He writes, "Christ also loved the church and gave Himself for her, that He might sanctify and cleanse her with the washing of water by the word…" Again, Scripture highlights the direct connection between the word and the process of cleansing or purification.

This is the same process in which we are "made clean" as Jesus' disciples today. The Scriptures are the purifying agent, working like a spiritual soap to cleanse our internal lives. Sanctification is a cleansing process, where we are stripped away of our dependence on self, learn to live free from sin's power and become conformed to the will and ways of God. As Merrill Tenney explains:

The means by which pruning or cleaning is done is by the Word of God. It condemns sin; it inspires holiness; it promotes growth. As Jesus applied the words God gave him to the lives of the disciples, they underwent a pruning process that removed evil from them and conditioned them for further service.²⁶

All of us need to submit ourselves to this purification as part of our training in the Crucified Lifestyle. Our interaction with the Bible is vital in this process as we embrace the truth and allow it to do its powerful work in our lives. The Word purifies us from the inside out and promotes spiritual maturity.

## DOING WHAT JESUS SAYS

Following a rabbi's teaching is the essence of what it means to be a disciple. One could say that discipleship is only truly taking place when the disciple is putting the teachings of the rabbi into practice. If a student was invited to follow a rabbi, but refused to do what he was instructed, the student-teacher relationship would be discontinued because discipleship cannot occur without a student's willingness to do what the rabbi taught. Obedience is the foundation of biblical discipleship.

A simple children's game provides a compelling illustration of discipleship. Most of us can recall playing the game "Simon Says" as children, which involves a group with an appointed leader, whose job it is to call out actions for the group to take. For example, the leader might say, "Simon says: Touch your nose! Simon says: Jump!" After each command is given, every other person in the group must perform the action, but only if the leader started the command with the words, "Simon says." If the command was only "Sit down!", whoever does that action must exit the game because Simon did not say to do it.

In John 14:15, Jesus gives His disciples a simple, but profound command: "If you love Me, keep My commandments." Sometimes, we tend to overcomplicate what it means to be a disciple of Christ. Put simply, discipleship is a real-life game of "Jesus says." If we do the things that our Rabbi commands us to do, and avoid doing what He tells us not to do, we will follow our Lord on His terms and thrive in our spiritual lives. We all need to regularly ask ourselves the questions, "Am I doing what my Master is telling me to do?" and "If not, why?" If we truly endeavor to obey the commands of Jesus found in the Word of God, then the process of spiritual maturity will happen organically.

The Crucified Lifestyle belongs to those who approach the Word of God with open hearts, ready to learn and willing to put it into practice. When we open the Bible, it is as if we are transported back into the first century and find ourselves sitting at the feet of our Rabbi, receiving and obeying His instruction. Even when the truth cuts deep, as it sometimes will, the one who wants to follow Christ wholeheartedly will be willing to allow the Word to pierce them "even to the division of soul and spirit, and of joints and marrow."[27] The result of that interaction with the Scriptures will be a more passionate, fruitful and surrendered life…the kind that Jesus desires all of His followers to enjoy.

The final spiritual discipline that we will discuss is by far the most important because without it, all of the other disciplines are meaningless. We will now examine the discipline of intimacy.

"To fall in love with God is the greatest romance; to seek him the greatest adventure; to find him, the greatest human achievement."

-Augustine[1]

# CHAPTER

# 11

## THE DISCIPLINE OF INTIMACY

*Crucified Christians Seek the Face of God Above All Else*

IN MANY CULTURES, WHEN A MAN and woman come together to pledge their lives in marriage, a token is exchanged. A wedding ring is symbolic of the spiritual union between a husband and wife. The gold ring I wear on my left hand is a physical representation of the deepest intimacy I have ever experienced with another human being. It is much more to me than a piece of jewelry; it speaks of my sincere lifetime commitment to be faithful to the vows I made to my wife to the best of my ability. If my ring could communicate words of its own, it would say, "I belong to my wife, and she belongs to me. I have chosen to spend the rest of my life loving and cherishing her."

The Lord has also given His people a deeply intimate gift. When we are born again, the Scripture teaches that the Holy Spirit takes up residence in us. Paul explains that the indwelling Holy Spirit is a deposit from the Lord telling us that we are His:

> He anointed us, set his seal of ownership on us, and put his Spirit in our hearts as a deposit, guaranteeing what is to come. **(2 Corinthians 1:21-22 NIV)**

> When you believed, you were marked in him with a seal, the promised Holy Spirit, who is a deposit guaranteeing our inheritance until the redemption of those who are God's possession—to the praise of his glory. **(Ephesians 1:13-14 NIV)**

I cannot think of a more intimate way for the Lord to prove that we belong to Him than to make us a dwelling place for His Spirit. As believers, we are literally hosts of the presence of God. Although this is a difficult concept for our minds to grasp, we have an experiential knowledge of His presence in our hearts. As Romans 8:16 explains, "The Spirit Himself bears witness with our spirit that we are children of God." Similar to a wedding ring, the Holy Spirit is a deeply intimate gift that bears the message, "Now you know that I am yours and you are Mine. I have chosen you to spend eternity with Me."

## WALKING WITH GOD

The human race was originally created to experience intimate relationship with God. In fact, before the Fall, Adam and Eve enjoyed unhindered intimacy with Him. We do not know how long they lived on the earth before they sinned the first time. But we do know that there was a duration of their lives when they walked with the Lord without the separation caused by sin. It is difficult to imagine what that must have been like, especially given the fallenness of the world in which we live. Scripture does not expound upon the details of Adam and Eve's relationship with God. We are only told that they spoke directly to God and that He walked "through the garden in the cool of the day."[2] I have often pondered what

ELEVEN: THE DISCIPLINE OF INTIMACY

the first two humans experienced. Walking beside someone is a relational activity and it creates an opportunity for heartfelt conversations. Amazingly, Adam and Eve had the opportunity to walk and talk with God Himself in the Garden of Eden.

I think about others in Scripture who walked closely with the Lord. One of the most fascinating stories comes from the Old Testament. A brief testimony is written in Genesis 5:24: "And Enoch walked with God; and he was not, for God took him." This one verse is packed with mystery. It tells us that there was once a man who did not die of natural causes but was taken from this life by the Lord. The writer of Hebrews later tells us that Enoch was taken by faith because he lived a life that pleased God.[3] What kind of relationship did Enoch have with the Lord that caused him to be taken this way? One can only imagine the depth of intimacy that he shared with God.

The disciples had the opportunity to literally walk with God in the flesh. In His three years of ministry, Jesus must have spent hundreds or even thousands of hours walking alongside His chosen Twelve. The Gospels capture only a limited amount of Jesus' interactions with them. This is because the Holy Spirit inspired the authors to record select scenes from His life so that future generations could learn about the Son of God and what He accomplished. But I often think about what was not written. For instance, what was it like to walk alongside Jesus? Can you imagine the long walking trips that they took together as they traveled throughout Israel on foot? Think about all the conversations that took place along the way. The disciples must have delighted in these daily walks with their Rabbi.

You and I will not have the ability to walk with God in this life the way that Adam and Eve did. Nor will we have the opportunity to walk alongside Jesus in the flesh as His disciples had. However, we do have access to the same intimacy that they enjoyed. And developing that kind of close relationship with God is the main purpose of the Crucified Lifestyle. And one of the most effective tools to foster intimacy in our relationship with the Lord is prayer.

# THE SOURCE OF SPIRITUAL LIFE

Prayer is the lifeblood of a Christian's relationship with the Lord. In the spiritual realm, prayer is similar to a baby's umbilical cord in its mother's womb. An umbilical cord is designed to pass nutrients along from a mother to her child during the gestation period. The human fetus needs these nutrients to develop and grow. Without this cord, the baby could not sustain life. Our prayer lives are like spiritual umbilical cords, where the grace, mercy and love of God are imparted to spiritually sustain us. If we neglect prayer, our passion for the Lord will fade because we are disconnecting ourselves from the source of our spiritual life.

When you depend on someone else for your very survival, a unique relationship is formed. A mother develops a special bond with her baby during pregnancy because of the process that occurs through the umbilical cord. My children will always have an attachment with my wife because they were literally connected to her for nine months. This is a picture of the relationship that we are to form with our Heavenly Father as we learn to be completely dependent on Him for everything we need. In this place of reliance on God, a deeply intimate bond is formed between us. Because of this, prayer and the Christian life are inseparable. As Martin Luther once said, "To be a Christian without prayer is no more possible than to be alive without breathing."[4]

# BUILDING RELATIONSHIP WITH GOD

Intimacy is a relational quality that comes from a deep heart-connection between two people. Synonyms of *intimacy* include terms like *belonging, closeness, familiarity* and *inseparability*. These qualities do not automatically develop in relationships but require time and intentionality. This is why building intimacy with God through prayer is something that must be pursued. The Bible uses several human relationships to describe the way God desires to interact with His people. Each of these provides a unique visual from our human experience about how we can relate to the Lord.

## *Friendship*

Friendships are a very important aspect of life. The quality and depth of these relationships are directly related to the time and effort poured into them. Casual friendships can be established relatively easily through common interests. However, stronger friendships must be developed and sustained through purposeful time spent together. Building trust and a deep connection in relationships requires much more than surface level discussions and experiences. Both parties must be fully invested in strengthening the friendship if it is to become healthy and strong. Each of these principles also apply to our relationship with God.

The concept of developing a friendship with Him is found in both the Old and New Testaments. God used the term *friend* when He spoke about His relationship with Abraham and Moses.[5] What a privilege to be called a personal friend of the Creator of the Universe! But these are not the only references of friendship with God in the Bible. In fact, Jesus uses similar language to describe His relationship with His disciples:

> No longer do I call you servants, for a servant does not know what his master is doing; but I have called you friends, for all things that I heard from My Father I have made known to you. (**John 15:15**)

We see in this verse that friendship with the Lord is not reserved for a few isolated people throughout history. All believers can develop the same close fellowship with God if we treat our relationship with Him like an important friendship that we want to pursue.

## *Marriage*

Marriage is a sacred commitment between two people that involves intimacy, trust and unconditional love. When a man and woman first fall in love, the couple embarks on an exciting journey of getting to know each other on a deeper level. In the beginning, spending time together seems effortless because of their newfound emotional attachment. However, a deeply committed marriage takes years of intentional effort, life experience and mutual contribution. As a couple chooses to pursue a stronger marriage, their relationship can develop into an intimate union unlike any other human bond.

Scripture uses this passionate human relationship to describe God's love for His people. In Isaiah, He is called Israel's husband.[6] The prophet Hosea's marriage is used as a natural illustration of God's spiritual marriage to His people.[7] Jesus and His church are referred to as a groom and bride in multiple passages.[8] Paul tells the church in Corinth that they have been married to Christ.[9] The Scriptures use this language to help us understand the rich intimacy and fierce loyalty that God wants to share with His people. Just like a healthy marriage requires firm commitment and determination, our relationship with God will only be as strong as our pursuit of Him.

*Parent and Child*

Another deeply intimate relationship that humans enjoy is the bond between a parent and a child. As a father of three girls, I can personally testify to the unconditional love that God has put in my heart for my daughters. The depth of my love for each of them is difficult to express with words. They are incredibly important to me, and I am so grateful that the Lord has entrusted my wife and I to steward their lives until adulthood. But even though we live under the same roof with our children, a strong relationship does not form without effort. The priority we place on spending time with them and sharing heartfelt communication has a substantial impact on the quality of our relationship with our kids.

As human parents, we love our children sincerely, yet imperfectly. Our sinful nature taints every relationship we have, even those closest to us. But the Scriptures speak about God as a good Father to His children. Jesus referred to Him as our perfect Heavenly Father.[10] We are told that we have been adopted into His family[11] and are therefore sons and daughters of God.[12] The love that the Father has for His children is unmatched by any earthly relationship. In fact, Jesus makes this radical statement in His prayer in John 17:23:

I in them, and You in Me; that they may be made perfect in one, and that the world may know that You have sent Me, and have loved them as You have loved Me.

Jesus asks God the Father to reveal to us that He loves us in the same way He loves Jesus. That might be hard for us to accept, especially considering how unlovable we may feel at times, but that is what Jesus is clearly expressing in His prayer. That rich love between the Father and His Son belongs to us. This truth is what leads the Apostle John to exclaim, "Behold what manner of love the Father has bestowed on us, that we should be called children of God!"[13] The Scriptures use the intimate love between a parent and child to describe the kind of relationship that is available between us and our Heavenly Father.

All human relationships develop and mature over time. Deliberate effort and investment are always required to form true intimacy with others. The same principles that we use to establish, strengthen and enjoy these important human relationships also assist us in our journey of getting to know God better. These include sharing daily experiences, having meaningful conversations, walking together through life's challenges, building trust and prioritizing our relationship with Him. Getting to know God personally is the single most important aspect of our lives. In fact, Jesus says in John 17:3 that eternal life is knowing God.

Although we may have some knowledge about God through His Word when we are first saved—our experiential knowledge grows over time. As we pursue the Lord in prayer, we discover more about who He is and develop a sensitivity to His voice. As Horatius Bonar encourages:

> Be much alone with God, and take time to get thoroughly acquainted. Converse over everything with Him. Unburden yourself wholly—every thought, feeling, wish, plan, doubt—to Him…He wants not merely to be on good terms with you, but to be intimate.[14]

## SEEKING AND FINDING

In Luke 15, Jesus shared the parable of the woman who lost a valuable coin. All of us can relate to her story when we think about losing something important to us. I experienced this in my own life recently. Our oldest daughter plays soccer in a very large complex and we were there one weekday evening to watch her game. When I went to work the next day, I reached into my pocket and realized that my flash drive containing very important digital files was missing. After searching in multiple locations, I finally concluded that it must have fallen out of my pocket somewhere in the soccer complex. I prayed for the Holy Spirit's guidance and drove to the deserted soccer facility. Miraculously within a few minutes, I was able to find it and I experienced the joy of receiving back something valuable that I had lost.

The parable of the lost coin is given between two other memorable parables: the lost sheep and the prodigal son. Jesus used all three of these stories to illustrate God's desire to search for lost people and also to reveal His great joy when they are found. Although these parables highlight the Father's heart to seek out His children, Scripture also tells us that God invites His people to seek and find Him.

Infinitely more thrilling than finding something material like a lost coin or valuable flash drive, is seeking and finding the Creator of heaven and earth! The Lord tells us in I Chronicles 28:9 that if we seek Him, He will be found by us. It is like a divine game of hide and seek that God likes to play with His children. And the reward is vastly greater than a feeling of excitement or relief; our reward is God Himself. Jeremiah 29:13 says, "You will seek Me and find Me, when you search for Me with all your heart." Notice that this is a conditional statement. We are not supposed to sit idly and wait for the Lord to come to us. Instead, we are all invited to intentionally search Him out with everything in us. Because of this, we should not treat time spent in prayer as something to check off a list so that we can move on to more important things, but as an exciting discovery of the God who created us and desires to have us as His own.

It is possible to develop such a life of prayer that we look forward to seeking the Lord. Although there will always be an element of discipline involved due to our flesh's resistance to prayer, the thrill of discovering more about Him should overshadow the distractions and difficulties. E.M. Bounds said it this way, "We regard prayer no longer as a duty which must be performed, but rather as a privilege which is to be enjoyed, a rare delight that is always revealing some new beauty."[15] When viewed in this context, prayer ceases to be a rote religious exercise and becomes a lifelong adventure of seeking and finding the One who made us.

## PRAYING LIKE JESUS

As followers of Christ, we are called to walk in the example that He left us, which includes a life of continual prayer. There are more than fifteen examples of Jesus praying to His Father in the Gospels.[16] We see Him praying in all different circumstances and situations, including the busiest seasons of His ministry. His prayers in the Garden of Gethsemane and even while hanging on the cross reveal that His response to crises was to cry out to His Father.[17] Although the Gospels do not detail every moment of Jesus' life, we can clearly see that He developed a routine habit of getting alone with God. The times of prayer recorded in the New Testament were not isolated events, but indicative of our Rabbi's lifestyle.

One example of Jesus' habit of prayer occurs after feeding a crowd of 5,000 men and their families. Matthew records that He did this with just five loaves of bread and two fish, an incredible miracle of multiplication. And the verses following this event tell us:

> Immediately Jesus made His disciples get into the boat and go before Him to the other side, while He sent the multitudes away. And when He had sent the multitudes away, He went up on the mountain by Himself to pray. (**Matthew 14:22-23**)

After spending this time in prayer, the chapter continues with the story of Jesus walking on the water. I find this passage of Scripture to be remarkable. The verse about Jesus going up on a mountainside to pray almost seems parenthetical to the story, as if Matthew is saying, "Here is some additional information wedged between two supernatural miracles." However, the significance of Jesus' time spent on that mountain cannot be overstated. The lesson to us should be simple and straight-forward: Jesus—who was God in the flesh—took time to get alone with God and pray, even when He was doing extraordinary miracles and drawing crowds of thousands to hear Him speak. If that is the example the Son of God set for us, how much more do we need to make time to do the same?

I have often wondered what that one-on-one prayer time was like between Jesus and His Father. Can you imagine the depth of that relationship? Can you picture what it was like for Him to commune with God, having never sinned and lived in perfect obedience every day of His life? Jesus lived with an unhindered intimacy with His Father. But this rich relationship is not reserved only for the Son of God during His brief journey on the earth. Instead, it is meant to be an example of the kind of relationship that is possible for us to enjoy if we too make it a habit to intentionally pursue God like He did. One way we can obey John's admonition to walk as Jesus walked[18] is to practice a lifestyle of intimate prayer.

## CEASELESS PRAYER

While I am a firm believer in having a substantial time of prayer in the morning hours, it can be helpful to think of prayer more like an ongoing conversation than a one-time event. Paul said in 1 Thessalonians 5:17 that we are to pray "without ceasing." Certainly, Paul could not be suggesting that we never leave our physical place of prayer. This would be impossible to obey because of the responsibilities that require our time and attention. We have relationships to maintain, jobs to work and families to raise. We have also been given the Great Commission,[19] which requires interaction with the world around us. None of these obligations can be fulfilled solely from our prayer closets. Instead, Paul is describing an intimate life in God in which we are inwardly communing with Him throughout our day. When we finish our time set aside for prayer in the morning, we should not be thinking, "Well Lord, I'll see you tomorrow morning," but rather, "Ok Father, let's go out and walk through this day together."

Psalm 105:4 tells us to seek God's face. Another translation of the word *face* is *presence*. To seek the face of God means that we are pressing into His presence. And there is nothing in this life that is more precious than the presence of God. One man who discovered the supreme value of God's presence was a friar in the seventeenth century named Brother Lawrence. He was most well-known for the letters he wrote that make up the book, "The Practice of the Presence of God." In this collection of writings, he describes how he trained himself to commune with the Lord at all times, even while doing menial tasks such as washing dishes. He describes the rich intimacy that was possible when he grew in his awareness of the presence of God. In his words:

> I make it my business only to persevere in His holy presence, where I keep myself by a simple attention, and a general fond regard to God, which I may call an actual presence of God; or, to speak better, an habitual, silent, and secret conversation of the soul with God, which often causes me joys and raptures inwardly, and sometimes also outwardly, so great that I am forced to use means to moderate them and prevent their appearance to others.[20]

To get to a place where we are continuously aware of the Lord may seem like an impossible task. But through discipline and intentionality, it is possible to teach our minds to focus on Him. This is why Brother Lawrence called it *practicing* God's presence. It is not something that our natural minds will do without training.

I have found this practice to be of great assistance in my own attempts to live the Crucified Lifestyle. I am often in situations that require me to make important decisions. When this happens, it is exceedingly helpful to have a quiet, internal conversation with the Lord. Sometimes, I am simply asking, "Jesus, what would you do if you were in my shoes right now?" Other times, I find myself in desperate need of His grace and I receive it through that secret place of continuous prayer. Staying in tune with the Holy Spirit is a discipline that takes time and effort, but the rewards of communing with Him throughout the day are worth the struggle. And as we develop the skill of listening and obeying Him, we will find ourselves increasingly living in the joy of the abundant life in Christ.

## PRAYER'S GREATEST ENEMY

Maintaining a disciplined and consistent prayer life is often a challenging task. This is not only because of the internal struggle with our flesh, but also because we are engaged in a spiritual battle. But this should come as no surprise. Prayer is very effective in developing intimacy in our relationship with God. Intimate prayer releases the presence and power of the Holy Spirit into our lives. His grace, mercy, love and anointing are all accessed through our intimate connection with the Lord. Intimacy is what makes the difference between powerless faith and the kind of faith that can move mountains. It is what prevents us from having a form of godliness but denying its power.[21] Satan is well aware of prayer's efficacy in fostering intimacy between us and the Lord, so he will do anything he can to prevent us from praying.

The Christian who strives to develop a vibrant prayer life will discover many obstacles that must be overcome. This is why it is of critical importance that we ardently protect our habit of prayer. To do so requires self-denial as we fight against lethargy, interruption, apathy and a host of other tactics that the enemy will throw at us. If he can defeat us in the prayer closet, he knows that he will be able to win the battle everywhere else. This is why Martyn Lloyd-Jones said, "Everything we do in the Christian life is easier than prayer."[22] We need to be diligent to persevere in prayer regardless of the pressure that will come against us. We have an enemy who will relentlessly attack us in an effort to discourage, distract and destroy our relationship with God. We will have seasons of grace when prayer seems to be effortless. But there will also be times when we need to fight persistently to maintain our life in God. In these difficult seasons, we must remind ourselves that this battle is well worth the effort. There is no greater prize than an intimate relationship with the Lord.

## A SAFEGUARD FROM LEGALISM

One reason that intimate prayer is necessary to live the Crucified Lifestyle is that the process of dying to self should never be done outside of a relational context. This is tremendously important to keep in mind as we endeavor to embrace the cross-life. To attempt to live this lifestyle outside of intimacy with the Lord will degrade our efforts into nothing more than legalistic attempts at spirituality. Intimacy is a safeguard that will help ensure that we approach the process of discipleship with proper motives.

Each of the practical principles that we have uncovered in this book is meant to be a relational exercise. Living free from the power of sin, the world system and the opinions of other people become realities as we pursue the Lord through intimate prayer. Surrendering our personal rights, plans and finances are all decisions that must be bathed in prayer. Fasting and interaction with the Scriptures are spiritual disciplines that find their greatest effectiveness when they are coupled with prayer. Trying to apply principles from a book without an intimate relationship with the Lord can easily become legalism. But everything taught in this book—when done from a place of sincere desire to please the Lord and develop a close relationship with Him—has the power to revolutionize our spiritual lives.

Cross-centered living is an ongoing process. All the lifestyle adjustments we have discussed must be prayed about, implemented and then prayed about even more. We should be in continual conversation with the Lord about every area of our lives, looking for His wisdom, guidance and direction. Intimacy will prevent our pursuit of the Crucified Lifestyle from becoming merely religious activity, and prayer is the gateway to that intimacy with the Lord.

## THE GREATEST BENEFIT OF DISCIPLESHIP

As I bring this chapter to a close, I want to remind us of Jesus' words from our main text: "If anyone desires to come after Me, let him deny himself, and take up his cross daily, and follow Me."[23] These words are meant to be an invitation into a deeply intimate walk with God. Too often, Christians have viewed this command from a negative perspective, considering what they will lose in the transaction. But there is no cost too high or sacrifice too great if the result is an increasing closeness with the God of the Universe. Therefore, the principle of disciplined intimacy from this chapter is the most important aspect of our response to Jesus' call to discipleship. Without intimacy, the Crucified Lifestyle becomes irrelevant.

Paul explains the connection of intimacy to our spiritual crucifixion in Galatians 2:20:

> I have been crucified with Christ; it is no longer I who live, but Christ lives in me; and the life which I now live in the flesh I live by faith in the Son of God, who loved me and gave Himself for me.

Herein lies both the primary purpose and reward of the Crucified Lifestyle. The cross is not only meant to be the death of our old lives, but an invitation into a rich union with Christ, who desires to live His life in and through us. Our willingness to die for Him is a direct response to His love and sacrifice for us. What a beautiful picture of the intimate relationship we can enjoy as a result of our desire to be crucified with Him! In the words of A.W. Tozer:

> The cross is rough, and it is deadly, but it is effective. It does not keep its victim hanging there forever. There comes a moment when its work is finished and the suffering victim dies. After that is resurrection glory and power, and the pain is forgotten for joy that the veil is taken away and we have entered in actual spiritual experience the Presence of the living God.[24]

May our hearts be reignited with a hunger for God and a passion for prayer that overshadows any resistance we may experience in our pursuit of intimacy with God.

"God hold us to that which drew us first, when the Cross was the attraction, and we wanted nothing else."

-Amy Carmichael[1]

# CONCLUSION

## THREE CROSS-CARRIERS

**A**S WE REVISIT OUR KEY PASSAGE from Luke 9 one last time, I pray that the meaning of this text has taken on new dimensions for you as we have progressed through this book. Once more, here is the invitational command given to us from our Savior's lips:

> If anyone desires to come after Me, let him deny himself, and take up his cross daily, and follow Me. (vs. 23)

These are the terms set by our Rabbi for all who seek to become His disciples. The question remains, "How will we respond to the truth of this verse?"

As we come to the end of our journey together, perhaps you may feel overwhelmed with the disparity between how much you have previously embraced the Crucified Lifestyle and your desire to do so in the future. Allow me to offer a few final thoughts that come from the stories of three people from Scripture who carried physical crosses during their lives.

**Simon Peter**

The first Cross-Carrier is the fisherman who left all behind to become a disciple of Christ: the Apostle Peter. The Gospel of Matthew records the moment when Jesus—walking along the Sea of Galilee—called Peter and his brother, Andrew, to become His disciples. He did so with a simple invitation: "Follow Me, and I will make you fishers of men."[2] In response, these two brothers immediately set down their fishing nets and embarked on their discipleship journey.

But Peter's attempt to follow Jesus was not without its failures. Earlier in Chapter 5, we referenced Peter's darkest moment that occurred on the night that Jesus was crucified. After his confident assertion that he would follow Jesus no matter what took place, Peter's faith was tested, and he wavered in the moment that it mattered most.[3] Rather than standing with Jesus in His time of greatest need, Peter denied knowing Him personally, not only once, but three times. When the reality of what he had done set in, Peter ran away, weeping bitterly with regret.[4]

After Jesus rose from the dead, He had a life-altering conversation with the downtrodden disciple. Jesus asked Peter three times about his love for Him. In that dialog, Peter was given an incredible gift: the opportunity to assert his love for Jesus once for each of his denials. It is a powerful depiction of restoration, as the Lord reassured Peter that he still had a place at the table. And then the Lord shared these words with Peter:

> "Most assuredly, I say to you, when you were younger, you girded yourself and walked where you wished; but when you are old, you will stretch out your hands, and another will gird you and carry *you* where you do not wish." This He spoke, signifying by what death he would glorify God. And when He had spoken this, He said to him, "Follow Me." **(John 21:18-19)**

Here, Jesus explained to Peter that a time would come when he would die a martyr's death on a literal cross. And history tells us that Peter was executed for his faith in an unusual way. Rather than a typical crucifixion, he was hung upside-down on a cross at his own request because he did not feel worthy to die in the same position as his Savior.[5] After revealing Peter's fate through these prophetic words, Jesus then spoke a phrase that had incredible significance in Peter's life. He extended the same invitation to him that he had at the very beginning of their relationship: "Follow me."

This was a defining moment in Peter's life. Despite his failures, Jesus' was still inviting him to follow as one of His disciples. He did not reject Peter and say, "It's too late. You've messed up too much. You are no longer qualified to be my disciple." Instead, He continued to beckon him into discipleship. The Book of Acts reveals that Peter responded to the call. And this time around, he proved his loyalty to Jesus, even when it led him to a physical death on a cross.

To all of us who have identified areas of failure in our own attempts to follow Jesus according to His terms in Luke 9:23, let us find encouragement in the fact that His invitation to follow is still offered to each of us. Even as you are reading these words, the Rabbi is beckoning you with the same offer that He spoke when He first called you: "Follow me." The only thing that can keep us from fully embracing the Crucified Lifestyle is our own stubborn refusal to respond to His invitation.

**Simon of Cyrene**

The second Cross-Carrier is a lesser-known Simon in the Scriptures. His brief encounter with Jesus appears in three of the Gospels, but Scripture provides very little information about this man from Cyrene. All we are told is that he was present at the moment Jesus was carrying His cross to the crucifixion site on the night of His death. We do not know why Simon was there along the pathway. But that day, he found his own story intertwined with one of the most famous stories of all time. Here are the verses describing the scene:

> Now as they came out, they found a man of Cyrene, Simon by name. Him they compelled to bear His cross. (**Matthew 27:32**)

> Then they compelled a certain man, Simon a Cyrenian, the father of Alexander and Rufus, as he was coming out of the country and passing by, to bear His cross. (**Mark 15:21**)

> Now as they led Him away, they laid hold of a certain man, Simon a Cyrenian, who was coming from the country, and on him they laid the cross that he might bear it after Jesus. (**Luke 23:26**)

Scripture does not disclose what was going through Simon's mind during this chaotic moment. Nor are we aware of any knowledge he might have had about Jesus prior to this event. But we can imagine what his reaction might have been to the scene unfolding in front of him. Asking Simon to carry the cross would be equivocal to asking a man to sit in an electric chair for a few minutes while they prepare a prisoner for execution or to tie a noose around his neck while they escort a condemned prisoner to the gallows. In all three passages, the Roman soldiers were the ones who initiated Simon's involvement in Jesus' cross-carrying journey. It was not as if Simon was overcome with compassion and volunteered to assist with the cross. In fact, Luke tells us that the soldiers "laid hold" of Simon. The other two Gospels use the word *compelled*. Both of these terms have the connotation of forcing Simon to carry the cross, most likely due to the fact that Jesus was so weak He could not continue to carry it Himself. Despite the likely fear of becoming a part of the crucifixion, Simon was not in a position to argue with the Roman soldiers who "compelled" him to take the cross from Jesus.

On the one hand, it is possible that this encounter with the Messiah may have dramatically changed the course of Simon's life. Perhaps he came to faith and chose to join ranks with the other disciples after encountering the Son of God firsthand. We simply have no other information from the Scriptures about what happened to the Cyrenian man. But his story does provide an illustration of those who make some attempt at living a cross-centered life—whether out of compulsion or religious duty—and yet, because they do not fully embrace the cross, they do not have the spiritual wherewithal to stay committed to the process of discipleship.

Simon had a cross on his back for a short period of time. But he had the luxury of handing it back over to the soldiers before the process was completed. He took the cross Jesus offered him, but only as long as needed, returning it to Him as soon as the chance presented itself. Simon's experience provides a picture of any attempt to live the Crucified Lifestyle from a place of comfort and convenience. The sacrifice that is required to embrace and apply the principles in this book is too great in the minds of those who are unwilling to carry the cross for the long haul. They love their own lives too much and their half-hearted attempts are not enough to motivate them to persevere through the seasons of struggle that are sure to come.

Some professing Christians agree with Luke 9:23 from an intellectual standpoint, but its truth never impacts their everyday lives. Others might respond to the invitation for a season, but never follow through because of the hardship and sacrifice required. Any effort at living the Crucified Lifestyle that does not involve all our hearts will not last until the end. Jesus is not looking for disciples who only follow when there is no personal cost to do so. His disciples are expected to carry their crosses until their last breath. In other words, we need to be all-in on the crucifixion life if we are going to experience the glory of the resurrection life.

**Jesus the Christ**

The third Cross-Carrier—who provides the best example of what it means to live the Crucified Lifestyle—is our Savior, Jesus Christ. A truth from the Scriptures caught my attention recently as I was reading through the Gospel of John. I came across a section that the editors titled, "The King on a Cross." In this chapter, John chronicled the final moments of Jesus' life on the earth. Pontius Pilate had just delivered Jesus to the soldiers to have Him crucified. And John 19:17 reads, "And He, bearing His cross, went out to a place called the Place of a Skull…" As I read those words, they seemed to jump off the page.

*"He, bearing His cross…"*

Just like so many other times throughout my faith journey, I was once again reminded of that old, rugged cross that our Savior took upon Himself. When I thought about that moment that John was describing, it dawned on me that Jesus is not asking us to do anything that He Himself was not willing to do. He is not inviting us to bear a cross that He has not already bore. And unlike Simon Peter, He never backed away from His assignment. He did pray for the Father to let the cup pass from Him in the Garden. But when God said "No," He embraced the cross for us.[6] And unlike Simon of Cyrene, He did not set the cross down in convenience or self-protection. He could have called on legions of angels to save Him, but He refused to exercise His rightful authority.[7] Instead, Scripture says, "For the joy set before Him…"[8] Our Savior did not have to do it, but love for the Father, and love for you and I, compelled Him to embrace the cross at the cost of His own life. And He has set the example of what it looks like to run the race set before us right through to the finish line.[9]

The place where Jesus was brought to be crucified was called Golgotha, which meant Skull Hill in Hebrew, due to the crucifixion site's resemblance to a human skull. The irony is that a place known for death was the same place God chose for eternal life to be procured. What looked like a terrible defeat in the natural was actually a pivotal moment for the greatest victory in history to occur. Death on the cross was a necessary element of the plan of salvation. But on the other side of the cross was resurrection life. It is the same for the Christian life. The abundant life that God has made available to each of us only comes through the work of the cross in our lives.

When we consider the Crucified Lifestyle, our flesh may cry out in protest, "This is unfair!" We may wrestle with the burden that comes from taking up this instrument of death upon our spiritual shoulders. But what right do any of us have to complain or question our Savior who died a violent death for our sins? How could we refuse to deny ourselves and fully surrender in light of the great sacrifice that He became so we could have eternal life? When we consider following Jesus from this perspective, it should be a great joy for us to walk through the sometimes painful process of discipleship.

We have covered many important topics in this book. Those who choose to live out the nine practical principles of cross-centered living that have been offered will undoubtedly be challenged to make both major and minor lifestyle changes. Those who endeavor to live a life that is crucified to sin, the world and the opinions of others; who choose to surrender their personal rights, plans and finances; and commit to engage with the disciplines of self-denial, maturity and intimacy, can only do so when the cross is embraced and applied to their lives wholeheartedly.

If you are left wondering how the Lord will ever manage to bring you into a life where all these principles are present, let me encourage you that you are in a good place. If we allow these truths to discourage us and cause us to cease striving to live the life of the cross, then the enemy of our souls will have won. However, the realization of our lack should cause us to simply lay ourselves at the feet of Jesus and put our faith in Him to do what we cannot do ourselves. If we can humbly do this, we are already further down the road than we may realize.

And now, fellow believer, the choice is yours. No one can make the decision for you. The journey is more than worthwhile and the pain is only temporary. Let us answer the calling that we have been given to enter into a life of discipleship on Jesus' terms. It is time for each of us to choose to deny ourselves, take up our cross and follow Him. May each person reading these words find themselves walking in the Crucified Lifestyle in increasing measure for the glory of God.

# APPENDIX

## THE PROCESS OF CRUCIFIXION

A proper understanding of the cross that Jesus was referring to in Luke 9:23 can be found in a historical study of Roman execution. Using crosses to slay criminals was a practice that dates back to the sixth century B.C. in ancient Persia. The Romans eventually adopted this practice as a form of capital punishment. Crucifixion was typically reserved for foreign criminals and people found guilty of insurrection. Roman citizens were most often excluded from this form of punishment. To provide us with some context of what the term *cross* represented at the time, let us walk alongside a prisoner condemned to death by the Romans on the day of his crucifixion to see what the process typically entailed. There were several forms of crucifixion practiced in the Roman Empire. For our purposes, we will focus on the form to which Jesus Himself was subjected.

When a prisoner was found guilty of a crime deemed worthy of crucifixion, he would be taken and scourged severely. The purpose of scourging was meant to bring the victim closer to death, hastening the crucifixion process. Often, the whips had pieces of metal and bone attached to them in order to produce as much pain and blood as possible.[1] Scourging would cause extreme pain and loss of blood and would often leave the prisoner in a state of shock. From this point, he would be forced to carry at least a crossbar to the crucifixion site. The fresh wounds on his back would cause excruciating pain as the crossbar rubbed across it, keeping the wounds open and blood flowing. But his agony was only beginning.

Once brought to the site of the crucifixion, the criminal would be nailed to the wooden cross in three strategic places in his body. One large spike would be driven into each wrist in a space between four carpal bones.[2] Another large spike was driven through his heels. These are areas of the human body that contain large nerve networks. The result of puncturing these pressure points would be a great deal of torturous pain inflicted upon the victim as he moved closer to his death. No doubt, the final minutes and hours of a crucified person's life were the most miserable and painful they would have ever experienced.

Once nailed to the cross, the deliberate positioning of the prisoner's body and the spikes driven through his wounds caused several things to occur simultaneously. There would be a great struggle in shifting his body weight to minimize the pain. The challenge for the person hanging on a cross was to balance his overwhelming pain with the severe difficulty of not being able to exhale fully. Although able to take shallow breaths in the hanging position, to get a full breath of air, the victim would have to push up with his feet. The stake in his heels would drive incredible pain into two major nerves in his legs. If the victim tried to relax to ease the pain of his feet and legs, his back would rub against the cross, reopening the wounds from the scourging. Also, the nerves in his wrists would send a jolt of pain throughout his body, and he would find himself unable to breathe. Eventually the victim would be so exhausted from the pain and blood loss that he would be unable to lift himself and he would suffocate.

If the Romans needed to accelerate the process, they would break the legs of the prisoner, forcing him into the final position that would hasten asphyxiation. This is what we see in the story of Jesus:

> Then the soldiers came and broke the legs of the first and of the other who was crucified with Him. But when they came to Jesus and saw that He was already dead, they did not break His legs. **(John 19:32-33)**

Of course, merely reading about crucifixion cannot cause us to truly grasp what an atrocious and agonizing death was involved in this form of capital punishment. Robert Gidley explained it this way:

> The Romans perfected crucifixion as a punishment designed to maximize pain and suffering. It wasn't about killing somebody—it was about killing somebody in a really horrible way. Someone who was crucified suffered the maximum amount of pain.[3]

When we examine the horrific procedure of crucifixion, it should cause a deep and fresh appreciation for what Jesus endured for us physically. Father God could have sent His Son at any other period in history when the death penalty would have been much less severe and drawn out. Jesus could have come and endured a firing squad, gas chamber, lethal injection, electric chair or have been hung on the gallows. Any of these methods would still have been an amazing sacrifice for us. However, Jesus chose to come to the earth at a time when He would experience one of the most horrid death penalties known in human history. What an awesome Savior! What an incredible sacrifice on our behalf!

# NOTES

**Opening Quotes**

1. A.W. Tozer. *The Crucified Life*. (Minneapolis, MN: Bethany House, 2011) p. 180.
2. Thomas á Kempis. *The Imitation of Christ*. (New York, NY: Penguin Putnam Inc, 1952) p. 83.

**Introduction**

1. Elisabeth Elliot. *These Strange Ashes*. (New York, NY: Harper & Row Publishers, 1975) p. 129.
2. John 10:10

**Chapter One: What Is the Crucified Lifestyle?**

1. Andrew Murray. *Humility*. (Springdale, PA: Whitaker House, 1982) p. 69.
2. See for examples: Matthew 9:14-15; Matthew 15:1-3; Mark 2:1-11; Mark 4:38-40; Mark 10:2-3; John 11:8-10
3. Matthew 13:13
4. James Strong. "New Strong's Concise Dictionary of the Words in the Greek Testament," T*he New Strong's Exhaustive Concordance of the Bible*. (Nashville, TN: Thomas Nelson Publishers, 1995) p. 99, ref. no. 5547.
5. James Strong. "New Strong's Concise Dictionary of the Words in the Hebrew Bible," *The New Strong's Exhaustive Concordance of the Bible*. (Nashville, TN: Thomas Nelson Publishers, 1995) p. 87, ref. no. 4899.

6. Matthew 2:1-18
7. Walter Kaiser. *The Promise-Plan of God: A Biblical Theology of the Old and New Testaments.* (Grand Rapids, MI: Zondervan, 2008) p. 327.
8. Joseph H. Thayer. *Thayer's Greek-English Lexicon of the New Testament.* (Grand Rapids, MI: 1977) p. 16, ref. no. 142.
9. A.W. Tozer. *The Radical Cross: Living the Passion of Christ.* (Camp Hill, PA: Wing Spread Publishers, 2009) pp. 3-4.
10. Vine, W.E. *The Expanded Vine's Expository Dictionary of New Testament Words.* Edited by John R. Kohlenberger III. (Minneapolis, MN: Bethany House Publishers, 1984) p. 284, ref. no. 720.
11. Murray W. Dempster, Byron D. Klaus and Douglas Petersen. *Called and Empowered.* (Peabody, MA: Hendrickson Publishers, Inc., 1991) p. 55.
12. Joseph H. Thayer. *Thayer's Greek-English Lexicon of the New Testament.* (Grand Rapids, MI: 1977) p. 22, ref. no. 191.
13. 1 John 4:8
14. Genesis 1:27
15. John 10:10
16. Hebrews 12:2 NIV
17. Matthew 19:22

**Chapter Two: The Path of Much Resistance**
1. Thomas á Kempis. *The Imitation of Christ.* (New York, NY: Penguin Putnam Inc, 1952) p. 86.
2. "Culture." *Merriam-Webster*, 2023. accessed online at https://www.merriam-webster.com/dictionary/culture.
3. James E. Plueddemann. *Leading Across Cultures.* (Downers Grove, IL: InterVarsity Press, 2009) p. 71.

4. "Paradox." *Oxford American Dictionary and Thesaurus.* (New York, NY: Oxford University Press, 2003) p. 1081.

5. Luke 12:15

6. Luke 9:23

7. "Will." *Oxford American Dictionary and Thesaurus.* (New York, NY: Oxford University Press, 2003) p. 1759.

8. Genesis 2:17

9. Philip M. Steyne. *In Step With the God of the Nations.* (Columbia, SC: Impact International Foundation, 1997) p. 49.

10. Matthew 26:39

11. John 1:14

12. Matthew 26:39

13. Matthew 4:1-11

14. Hebrews 4:15

15. Steve Gallagher. *Irresistible to God.* (Dry Ridge, KY: Steve Gallagher, 2003) p. 108.

16. John 14:15

17. James Strong. "New Strong's Concise Dictionary of the Words in the Greek Testament," *The New Strong's Exhaustive Concordance of the Bible.* (Nashville, TN: Thomas Nelson Publishers, 1995) p. 39, ref. no. 2218.

**Section Two: A Victorious Lifestyle**

1. "Victory." *Oxford American Dictionary and Thesaurus.* (New York, NY: Oxford University Press, 2003) p. 1714.

**Chapter Three: Crucified to Sin**

1. Charles Spurgeon. *Spurgeon's Sermons: The Metropolitan Tabernacle Pulpit, Vol. 15.* (Classic Christian Library, 1869) p. 686. http://www.mediafire.com/file/rm5idnfhd54qic5/Spurgeon-Metropolitan-pt15.pdf/file. PDF File.

2. See Revelation 21:4; 21:27; 22:15
3. Ephesians 1:14 NIV
4. Joseph H. Thayer. *Thayer's Greek-English Lexicon of the New Testament.* (Grand Rapids, MI: 1977) p. 379, ref. no. 3049.
5. Acts 9
6. Acts 22:3
7. Acts 7:58
8. Acts 8:3
9. Walter C. Kaiser, Jr. *The Promise-Plan of God: A Biblical Theology of the Old and New Testaments.* (Grand Rapids, MI: Zondervan, 2008) p. 258.
10. Robert H. Mounce. *The New American Commentary: Romans.* (Brentwood, TN: Broadman & Holman Publishers, 1995) p. 167.
11. Robert H. Mounce. *The New American Commentary: Romans.* (Brentwood, TN: Broadman & Holman Publishers, 1995) p. 166.
12. Source Unknown
13. Romans 6:11

**Chapter Four: Crucified to the World**

1. Mark K. Olson. *John Wesley's 'A Plain Account of Christian Perfection,' The Annotated Edition.* (Fenwick, MI: Alethea in Heart, 2006) p. 238.
2. "Legalism." *New Webster's Dictionary and Thesaurus of the English Language.* (Danbury, CT: Lexicon Publications, Inc., 1993) p. 565.
3. Matthew 5:14
4. 2 Corinthians 6:14 NIV
5. *Hebrew-Greek Key Word Study Bible.* NIV. "Lexical Aids to the New Testament." (Chattanooga, TN: AMG Publishers, 1996) p. 1642, ref. no. 3180.

6. Steve Gallagher. *Intoxicated with Babylon*. (Dry Ridge, KY: Steve Gallagher, 2006) p. 22.

7. "Worldview." *Merriam-Webster*, 2023. accessed online at https://www.merriam-webster.com/dictionary/ worldview.

8. "Humanism." *Merriam-Webster*, 2023. accessed online at https://www.merriam-webster.com/dictionary/humanism.

9. "Atheism." *Merriam-Webster*, 2023. accessed online at https://www.merriam-webster.com/dictionary/atheism.

10. "Hedonism." *Merriam-Webster*, 2023. accessed online at https://www.merriam-webster.com/dictionary/hedonism.

11. Ecclesiastes 8:15

12. Andrew Bonar, as cited in *Intoxicated with Babylon*, by Steve Gallagher. (Dry Ridge, KY: Steve Gallagher, 2006) p. 17.

13. Hannah Whitall Smith. T*he Christian's Secret of a Happy Life: A Modern Abridgment*. (Uhrichsville, OH: Barbour Publishing, Inc., 1986) p. 74.

14. Watchman Nee. *Love Not the World*. (Fort Washington, PA: Christian Literature Crusade, 1971) p. 16.

15. Romans 12:2

16. Bible Hub. "suschématizó." *Discovery Bible*, 2021. Accessed online at https://biblehub.com/greek/4964.htm.

17. "Martin Quigley, Wrote Film Code; Co-Author of Production Guide, a Publisher, Dies." *The New York Times*, 5 May 1964, www.nytimes.com/1964/05/05/archives/martin-quigley-wrote-film-code-coauthor-of-production-guide-a.html. Accessed 1 November 2023.

18. Colossians 3:2

19. "Time Flies: U.S. Adults Now Spend Nearly Half a Day Interacting with Media." *The Nielson Company*, July 2018, www.nielsen.com/us/en/insights/article/2018/time-flies-us-adults-now-spend-nearly-half-a-day-interacting-with-media. Accessed 7 June 2023.

20. Jamie Friedlander Serrano. "Experts Can't Agree on How Much Screen Time Is Too Much for Adults." *Time*, 9 May 2022, www.time.com/6174510/how-much-screen-time-is-too-much. Accessed 1 November 2023.

21. Romans 14:12

22. Matthew 12:36

23. Hebrews 12:14 NIV

24. G. D. Watson. "Others May, You Cannot." *Bible.org*, 2 February 2009, https://bible.org/illustration/others-may-you-cannot. Accessed 1 November 2023.

25. Philippians 4:8 NIV

26. Andrew Murray. *The Ministry of Intercession*. (Alresford, Hants: Marshall Morgan & Scott, 1981) p. 129.

**Chapter Five: Crucified to the Opinions of People**

1. William Gurnall. As cited online, quote accessed at: https://gracequotes.org/author-quote/william-gurnall.

2. "Fear." *Merriam-Webster*, 2023. accessed online at https://www.merriam-webster.com/dictionary/fear.

3. Matthew 10:22

4. Galatians 1:10 NIV

5. Bible Hub. "moquesh." *Strong's Exhaustive Concordance*, 2023. Accessed online https://biblehub.com/hebrew/4170.htm.

6. Jeremiah 1:19 NIV

7. Jeremiah 11:18-23

8. Marie Gentert King. *Foxe's Book of Martyrs*. (Old Tappan, NJ: Fleming H. Revell Company, 1970) p. 12.

9. Matthew 26:35 NLT

10. Matthew 26:69-75

11. See Acts 10 and 11; Romans 11:13; Galatians 1:15-16

12. Acts 2:41
13. Revelation 2:4-5
14. T.F. Tenney. as cited online, quote accessed at: https://www.sermoncentral.com/sermons/how-far-do-you-want-to-go-jeff-strite- sermon-on-fear-256619.
15. Leonard Ravenhill. as cited online, quote accessed at: https://www.sermonindex.net/modules/myalbum/photo.php?lid=906.
16. Galatians 4:16
17. 2 Corinthians 11:23-27

**Section Three: A Surrendered Lifestyle**

1. "Surrender." *New Webster's Dictionary and Thesaurus of the English Language*. (Danbury, CT: Lexicon Publications, Inc., 1993) p. 996.
2. Romans 8:7 NIV

**Chapter Six: Surrendering Our Personal Rights**

1. Oswald Chambers. as cited online, quote accessed at: https://www.azquotes.com/quote/724049.
2. A.W. Tozer. *The Best of A.W. Tozer, Book Two*. (Camp Hill, PA: Baker House Book Company, 1980) p. 151.
3. John 8:34; 1 John 5:19
4. 2 Timothy 2:3-4
5. A.W. Tozer. *The Radical Cross: Living the Passion of Christ*. (Camp Hill, PA: Wing Spread Publishers, 2009) pg. 100.
6. Hudson Taylor, as cited in "Lessons in Discipleship" by Roger Steer. *OMF International*, 1995. p. 34. accessed online at: https://omf.org/us/about/our-story/quotes.
7. "All to Jesus I Surrender." as cited online, accessed at: https://hymnary.org/text/all_to_jesus_i_surrender

8. Galatians 5:16
9. Deitrich Bonhoeffer. *The Cost of Discipleship*. (New York, NY: Touchstone, 1995) p. 89.
10. 1 John 2:6
11. Philippians 2:6 NIV
12. Philippians 2:7 NIV
13. Philippians 2:8
14. Elisabeth Elliot. Laying Down Our Rights, 2018. as cited online, accessed at: https://www.reviveourhearts.com/podcast/revive-our-hearts/will-you-lay-down-your-rights-1.
15. "Revenge." *Cambridge Dictionary*, 2023. Accessed online at https://dictionary.cambridge.org/us/dictionary/english/revenge.
16. Luke 23:34
17. Matthew 6:15
18. Colossians 3:13 NIV
19. 1 Peter 2:11
20. Romans 12:2
21. Galatians 5:17
22. 1 Peter 4:2
23. Philippians 2:14
24. Philippians 4:4
25. James 1:2
26. John of the Cross. as cited online, quote accessed at: https://www.azquotes.com/quote/568515.
27. Luke 3:19-20
28. Philippians 4:19
29. 1 John 5:14-15
30. 2 Timothy 2:13

31. Steve Gallagher. *Standing Firm Through the Great Apostasy*. (Dry Ridge, KY: Steve Gallagher, 2008) pp. 30-33.

**Chapter Seven: Surrendering Our Plans**

1. George MacDonald. As cited online, quote accessed at: https://www.azquotes.com/quote/182159.
2. Proverbs 15:22; 16:1, 3, 9; 21:5
3. 1 Corinthians 12:17-19
4. Luke 14:11
5. See for examples: Luke 9:46; 22:24; Matthew 18:1; Mark 10:37
6. Genesis 37:5
7. Genesis 17:19
8. Genesis 12:7; 17:4, 19
9. Genesis 22:3
10. Genesis 22:12

**Chapter Eight: Surrendering Our Finances**

1. George Muller. *The Autobiography of George Muller*. (Springdale, PA: Whitaker House, 1984) p. 212.
2. 1 Timothy 6:10
3. Matthew 6:21
4. "Steward." *Collins Dictionary*, 2023. Accessed online at https://www.collinsdictionary.com/us/dictionary/english/steward.
5. James 1:17
6. Deuteronomy 8:18
7. Matthew 6:20
8. *Hebrew-Greek Key Word Study Bible*. NIV. "A Concise Dictionary of the Hebrew." (Chattanooga, TN: AMG Publishers, 1996) p. 1970, ref. no. 5130.

9. Genesis 28:20-22
10. Malachi 3:8-11
11. Hebrews 7:9
12. See Leviticus 1 and 6
13. See Leviticus 22 and 23
14. Bible Hub. "hilaros." *Discovery Bible*, 2021. Accessed online at https://biblehub.com/greek/2431.htm.

## Section Four: A Disciplined Lifestyle

### Chapter Nine: The Discipline of Self-Denial

1. Watchman Nee. *The Spiritual Man.* (New York, NY: Christian Fellowship Publishers, Inc., 1968) p. 429.
2. Bible Hub. "arneomai." *New American Standard Exhaustive Concordance*, 1998. Accessed online at https://biblehub.com/greek/720.htm.
3. Psalm 139:14 NIV
4. Bible Hub. "sarx." *Discovery Bible*, 2021. Accessed online at https://biblehub.com/greek/4561.htm.
5. Robert South. *Sermons Preached Upon Several Occasion, Vol. VII.* (Oxford, England: Clarendon Press, 1823) p. 180-181.
6. Romans 8:29
7. Gottfried Osei-Mensah. *Wanted: Servant Leaders.* (Hong Kong: Christian Communications, Ltd., 1990) p. 48-49.
8. Ofer Amitai, spoken during his message at the Pure Life Annual Conference on April 28-29. 2023 at the Ark Encounter in Williamstown, KY.
9. Bible Hub. "apekduomai." *Discovery Bible*, 2021. Accessed online at https://biblehub.com/greek/554.htm.

10. Robert H. Mounce. *The New American Commentary: Romans.* (Brentwood, TN: Broadman & Holman Publishers, 1995) p. 153.

11. Galatians 6:8

12. Robert South. *Sermons Preached Upon Several Occasion, Vol. VII.* (Oxford, England: Clarendon Press, 1823) p. 191-192.

13. See Leviticus 2:9; Numbers 29:2

14. C.S. Lewis. *Mere Christianity, Fiftieth Anniversary Edition.* (Glasgow, England: Omnia Books, Ltd., 1952) p. 191-192.

**Chapter Ten: The Discipline of Maturity**

1. Oswald Chambers. *My Utmost for His Highest, The Classic Edition.* (Uhrichsville, OH: Barbour Publishing, Inc., 1963) p. 46.

2. Ray Vander Laan. "Synagogue School." *That the World May Know.* Accesed online at https://www.thattheworldmayknow.com/synagogue-school.

3. Ray Vander Laan. "Rabbi and Talmidim." *That the World May Know.* Accesed online at https://www.thattheworldmayknow.com/rabbi-and-talmidim.

4. Joseph H. Thayer. *Thayer's Greek-English Lexicon of the New Testament.* (Grand Rapids, MI: 1977) p. 22, ref. no. 190.

5. See for examples: Matthew 4:19, 9:9; Mark 1:17

6. Edgar Elliston. *Home Grown Leaders.* (Pasadena, CA: William Carey Library, 1992) p. 76-77.

7. Colossians 1:15

8. 2 Corinthians 4:4

9. Bible Hub. "eikón." *Discovery Bible*, 2021. Accessed online at https://biblehub.com/greek/1504.htm.

10. Bible Hub. "metamorphoó." *Discovery Bible*, 2021. Accessed online at https://biblehub.com/greek/3339.htm.

11. Bible Hub. "sýmmorphos." *Discovery Bible*, 2021. Accessed online at https://biblehub.com/greek/4832.htm.

12. Acts 4:13 NIV
13. Romans 12:2
14. Bible Hub. "diaskalia." *Discovery Bible*, 2021. Accessed online at https://biblehub.com/greek/1319.htm.
15. James 1:22
16. Joseph H. Thayer. *Thayer's Greek-English Lexicon of the New Testament*. (Grand Rapids, MI: 1977) p. 202-203, ref. no. 1651.
17. Joseph H. Thayer. *Thayer's Greek-English Lexicon of the New Testament*. (Grand Rapids, MI: 1977) p. 228, ref. no. 1882.
18. Joseph H. Thayer. *Thayer's Greek-English Lexicon of the New Testament*. (Grand Rapids, MI: 1977) p. 473, ref. no. 3809.
19. Bible Hub. "eksartizo." *Discovery Bible*, 2021. Accessed online at https://biblehub.com/greek/1822.htm.
20. 1 Peter 2:2
21. Hebrews 5:13
22. Joseph H. Thayer. *Thayer's Greek-English Lexicon of the New Testament*. (Grand Rapids, MI: 1977) p. 399, ref. no. 3306.
23. Edgar Elliston. *Home Grown Leaders*. (Pasadena, CA: William Carey Library, 1992) p. 104.
24. Bible Hub. "katharós." *Discovery Bible*, 2021. Accessed online at https://biblehub.com/greek/2513.htm.
25. Joseph H. Thayer. *Thayer's Greek-English Lexicon of the New Testament*. (Grand Rapids, MI: 1977) p. 6, ref. no. 37.
26. *Enduring Word*. "John 15:1-3." Merrill Tenney, as cited online, quote accessed at: https://enduringword.com/bible-commentary/john-15.
27. Hebrews 4:12

## Chapter Eleven: The Discipline of Intimacy

1. Augustine. As cited online, quote accessed at: https://www.azquotes.com/quote/363375.

2. Genesis 3:9
3. Hebrews 11:5
4. Martin Luther. As cited online, quote accessed at: https://www.azquotes.com/quote/544784.
5. See verses: II Chronicles 20:7; Isaiah 41:8; James 2:23; Exodus 33:11
6. See verses: Hosea 2:16; Jeremiah 31:32; Isaiah 54:5
7. Hosea 1 and 3
8. See verses: Revelation 21:2; Matthew 9:15; John 3:29
9. 2 Corinthians 11:2
10. Matthew 5:48
11. See verses: Ephesians 1:5; Romans 8:15; Romans 8:23; Galatians 4:5
12. See verses: John 1:12; Galatians 3:26; 2 Corinthians 6:18
13. 1 John 3:1
14. Horatius Bonar. As cited online, quote accessed at: https://www.azquotes.com/quote/662218.
15. E.M. Bounds. As cited online, quote accessed at: https://www.azquotes.com/quote/550432.
16. See for examples: Luke 3:21; Matthew 14:23; Mark 6:46; Luke 6:12
17. Matthew 26:39 and Luke 23:34
18. 1 John 2:6
19. Matthew 28:16–20
20. Brother Lawrence. *The Practice of the Presence of God*. (Uhrichsville, OH: Barbour Publishing, Inc., 2004) p. 39.
21. 2 Timothy 3:5
22. Martyn Lloyd-Jones. As cited online, quote accessed at: https://gracequotes.org/author-quote/martyn-lloyd-jones.
23. Luke 9:23

24. A.W. Tozer. *The Pursuit of God*. (Vancouver, Canada: Eremitical Press, 1948) p. 42.

**Conclusion**

1. Amy Carmichael. As cited online, quote accessed at: https://www.azquotes.com/quote/437296.
2. Matthew 4:19
3. Luke 22:54-62
4. Luke 22:62
5. Marie Gentert King. *Foxe's Book of Martyrs*. (Old Tappan, NJ: Fleming H. Revell Company, 1970) p. 12.
6. Matthew 26:44-46
7. Matthew 26:53
8. Hebrews 12:2 NIV
9. Hebrews 12:1-3

**Appendix**

1. Bible Hub. "Matthew 27:26." *Ellicott's Commentary of English Readers, Gill's Exposition of the Entire Bible, Pulpit Commentary,* 2023. Accessed online at https://biblehub.com/commentaries/matthew/27-26.htm.
2. Cahleen Shrier, Ph.D. "The Science of the Crucifixion." *Asuza Pacific University*, 2002. Accessed online at https://www.apu.edu/articles/the-science-of-the-crucifixion.
3. Robert Gidley. "The Facts of Crucifixion." *Catholic Education Resource Center*, 2000. Accessed online at https://www.catholiceducation.org/en/controversy/common-misconceptions/the-facts-of-crucifixion.html.

# ABOUT THE AUTHOR

Dustin Renz is the founder of Make Way Ministries. He holds a Bachelor of Science in Church Ministries from Southeastern University in Lakeland, Florida. He currently serves as a missionary-evangelist and the President of Make Way Ministries. He also serves as a speaker for Pure Life Ministries in Dry Ridge, Kentucky. He is the author of *Pile of Masks: Exposing Christian Hypocrisy* and the evangelistic novel, *Something Better*. He and his wife, Brittany, have three wonderful daughters and they currently reside in Kettering, Ohio.

Make Way Ministries was established with the purpose of empowering the Body of Christ to awaken in revival, mature through discipleship and arise to evangelism as we make way for our soon-coming King, Jesus Christ. We accomplish this through our speaking, publishing and online ministries.

For more information about booking an event or to find resources, please visit us at www.makewayministries.com or email us at: contact@makewayministries.com

# PILE of MASKS

## LEARN HOW TO LIVE WITH AN UNDIVIDED HEART!

Have you ever wondered why hypocrisy is so prevalent in the church? Many people have rejected the Christian faith due to the fact that they see nothing different in the lives of those who profess Christ and the rest of the world. The church is filled with the same issues that they face such as high divorce rates, drug and alcohol abuse, relational conflict, sexual immorality, fear of the future and an obsession with the things of this world. Is there any hope for a church culture that has grown lukewarm in its love for Jesus?

In Pile of Masks, Dustin Renz candidly explores this issue in the Christian community from an insider's vantage point. Having been set free from a hypocritical lifestyle himself, he explains how the Lord broke the chains of hypocrisy in his heart, restored his marriage and ministry and brought him into an authentic life in Christ.

This book takes readers on a journey through history to discover how the enemy has been using hypocrisy to pull people away from God since the beginning of time. It presents powerful principles to help all believers rise above a backslidden church culture. All who hunger for more than status quo Christianity need to read this book!

WWW.MAKEWAYMINISTRIES.COM

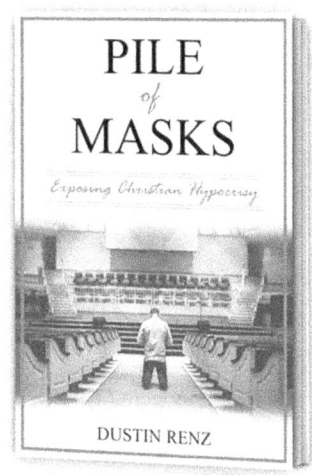 

**WHAT OTHERS ARE SAYING ABOUT *PILE OF MASKS*:**

"Introspectively challenges your walk with Christ."
-**Ken Hathcoat (Amazon Review)**

"Filled with Biblical truth and an in-depth understanding of how a personal relationship with Jesus Christ sets us free. I found it to be life-changing and helpful for those who apply God's Word to walk in truth and lay down the mask of hypocrisy."
-**Scott F. (Amazon Review)**

"Brilliantly reveals the problem and 'exposes' it like few others."
-**David Frazier (Amazon Review)**

"Pile of Masks is an in-depth, Biblical look at hypocrisy and the path to deliverance. It is hard to put this book down; It is eye opening, heart wrenching, and life changing. I am so grateful to the Lord for this book."
-**Dan Nieves (Amazon Review)**

# The PILE of MASKS
## *Teaching Series*

**NOW AVAILABLE as a Video Series!**

- 13 sessions from the book that is helping Christians find freedom from hypocrisy
- Over 4.5 hours of teaching
- Recorded in the Pure Life Ministries Chapel

WWW.MAKEWAYMINISTRIES.COM OR
WWW.YOUTUBE.COM/MAKEWAYMINISTRIES

# SOMETHING BETTER

He's lost his way and his family. Can a leap of faith bring them back together?

Tom Schneider's inner demons have cost him dearly. Still emotionally scarred from his abusive childhood, he fears he may never be the supportive husband and parent his family needs. After his wife takes their daughter and leaves, he wallows in his pain until his estranged father reaches out with a final dying wish.

Coping with his trauma and hopelessness, he returns to his Southern hometown in search of redemption. As he takes the winding path to self-discovery, he finds solace in a local church. But it's a chance encounter that might just renew his faith in a brighter future.

Will Tom forgive the sins of his past and open his heart to happiness?

*Something Better* is an inspirational Christian fiction story about the transformational power of redemption. If you like flawed heroes, tests of faith, and heartwarming journeys of rebirth, then you'll love Dustin Renz's second-chance saga.

WWW.MAKEWAYMINISTRIES.COM

## WHAT OTHERS ARE SAYING ABOUT *SOMETHING BETTER:*

"Renz has beautifully imagined a redemption story with believable characters. Strongly recommended!"

-(Goodreads Review)

"The biblical message is strong as the main character discovers how real Jesus really is. A very hopeful book. I highly recommend it!"

-Christy (Amazon Review)

"What an incredible story of the path and power of redemption."

-Cinthia (Amazon Review)

"So many books are forgettable, but this one will stay with me a while. Tom's experience is so close to what I went through coming to Christ, and the broken and redeemed marriage is so familiar. Renz made his characters resonate with reality. Not many stories bring tears, but this one did."

-Tenney Singer (Amazon Review)

# REAPING A SPIRITUAL HARVEST

*Rekindle the passion in your devotional life!*

Reaping a Spiritual Harvest is a unique devotional tool. The first part contains a study on the biblical principle of sowing and reaping, specifically as it applies to our spiritual lives. The second part of the book contains an interactive 21-page Spiritual Diagnostic Tool. This journaling section comes complete with fill-in-the blanks, scales, question and answers and Scripture passage studies.

The primary purpose of the study is to connect the sowing and reaping process with the spiritual disciplines. Six specific disciplines are considered, including Prayer, Interaction with Scripture, Fasting, Worship, Financial Stewardship and Evangelism. Each discipline has worksheet pages with Examine, Envision and Engage sections to help believers discover their strengths and weaknesses in each discipline and make practical changes to engage with these spiritual disciplines more effectively.

WWW.MAKEWAYMINISTRIES.COM

## AVAILABLE IN PAPER AND DIGITAL FORMAT!

# Connect with us

 www.makewayministries.com

 Facebook.com/makewayministries

 YouTube.com/makewayministries

 @makewaymin

 @make_way_ministries

 contact@makewayministries.com

www.ingramcontent.com/pod-product-compliance
Lightning Source LLC
Chambersburg PA
CBHW050327010526
44119CB00050B/710